FORM AN

CW00732961

FORM AND MATTER

THEMES IN CONTEMPORARY METAPHYSICS

Edited by

David S. Oderberg

BLACKWELL
Publishers

Copyright © Blackwell Publishers Ltd 1999

ISBN 0 631 21389 9

First published 1999

Blackwell Publishers
108 Cowley Road, Oxford OX4 1JF, UK.
and
350 Main Street,
Malden, MA 02148, USA.

British Library Cataloguing in Publication Data

A catalogue record for this book is available from the
British Library.

Library of Congress Cataloging in Publication Data

Available from the publisher

Typeset by Cambrian Typesetters, Frimley, Surrey
Printed in Great Britain by Whitstable Litho, Kent
This book is printed on acid-free paper

CONTENTS

INTRODUCTION

Recent years have seen a welcome revival of interest in Aristotelian philosophy. I say 'Aristotelian philosophy' rather than 'the philosophy of Aristotle' because the latter would suggest that the revival is primarily historical or exegetical in character. It is true that much interesting scholarly work is being done on the interpretation of the man whom St. Thomas Aquinas, among other thinkers of the Middle Ages, called simply 'the Philosopher'. Impressive work has been done, for instance, on his critique of Plato's theory of Ideas, and on his philosophy of biology. Equally impressive and in my opinion more important work, however, is being done in the Aristotelian *tradition*. Rather than concentrating on the niceties of Aristotelian exegesis – important though they be – a growing number of philosophers, influenced by Aristotelianism itself, are seeking ways of applying it to a range of problems, some novel, others venerable albeit expressed in contemporary terms.

This regrowth of Aristotelianism, though still in its early stages, should be seen as a welcome corrective to some dominant modern trends. Perhaps the most prominent is the *reductionism* which permeates so much of contemporary philosophy, and which can be loosely characterized as an incessant drive to explain reality in terms of the fewest possible fundamental concepts. Coupled with the prevailing *nominalism*, the idea that reality is explained essentially in terms of human beings' mental and linguistic operations rather than in terms of objects which lie outside the mind in categories which are not *invented* but *discovered*, the result is that recent philosophy has taken a decidedly sceptical and inward turn.

On the other hand, there have been hints of a return of Platonism. It is true that the extent to which Aristotle's own philosophy is imbued with elements of Platonic thinking (as opposed to being exclusively a reaction against it) has been mostly underestimated, and recent exegesis is again pointing the way to a more balanced understanding of the relation between these two masters. It remains true, nevertheless, that there is a fundamental incompatibility between the stances of

Aristotelianism and Platonism, understood primarily in terms of whether the explanation of concrete physical reality is, as it were, wholly 'other-worldly' or not. Given the manifest and complete 'this-worldliness' of most of contemporary philosophy, it is understandable that some philosophers, rightly dissatisfied with such an approach, should begin to look in Plato's direction for a remedy. And yet the traditional objections to Platonism – in particular concerning its inability to give a satisfying account of the explanatory relationship between the 'this-worldly' and the 'other-worldly' – will not go lightly. Hence the essential healthiness of a return to the traditional *via media* – Aristotelianism.

It is in metaphysics that the revived influence of Aristotle is most prominent. This should not be surprising, because it is in the Aristotelian tradition that the primacy of metaphysics above all other fields of philosophy is most insisted upon. This is certainly the case by contrast with the dominance in contemporary thought of epistemology and the philosophy of mind, where the emphasis is far less on what there is than upon how we can begin to think about working out how we might just be able to know something of what there is – the incessant 'spectacle cleaning' so derided by Karl Popper. Aristotelianism begins unashamedly with *being*, not with the mind, or language, or knowledge, or opinion, or paradox. To be sure, it embraces all of these, but it first puts them in their rightful place, as phenomena which must be explained in terms of the fundamental categories of being, which categories are not mere products of human invention, or inescapable presuppositions of all knowledge, but the very fabric of the universe itself. The Aristotelian begins with being – and ends with being – and explains everything else in terms of the multifarious *kinds* of being which go to make up the whole of reality. Metaphysics, as 'queen of philosophy', as 'first philosophy' (to use Aristotle's term) is, then, the obligatory starting point for all who would call themselves Aristotelians.

Since the concepts of *form* and *matter* are at the very root of Aristotelian thinking, the title for the volume suggested itself. All of the contributors, in one way or another, discuss form and matter, but their interests and concerns are as diverse as Aristotle's own. (Since each paper begins with an abstract, I will not summarize them here, as opposed to making some brief comments.) Jonathan Lowe examines the central Aristotelian doctrine of *hylomorphism*, that every individual concrete thing is a combination of matter and form. Noting the apparent tension between early and late Aristotle on the role of this doctrine in the analysis of *substance*, he proposes a reconciliation based on an *identification* of individual concrete things (the 'primary substances' of Aristotle's *Categories*) with particular substantial forms (the primary substances of Aristotle's *Metaphysics*), leading to the conclusion that there is nothing absurd in the notion of *form without matter*, and that perhaps fundamental physical particles, as well as individual *persons*, exemplify such a notion.

Peter Simons, too, is concerned with the analysis of substance. He discerns various strands in metaphysical thinking about just what substance is, and points out that this lack of a unitary concept is arguably traceable back to Aristotle himself. On the other hand he, like Aristotle, wishes to defend an 'everyday concept' of substance, whose instances differ from things such as events, processes, qualities and relations, and endure through time and change. It would, he says, require a 'conceptual revolution of unprecedented magnitude' to remove or replace this everyday notion of substance. Where Simons differs from Aristotle, however, is in arguing that everyday substances are not *primitive*: they 'may perhaps, as Aristotle says, be prior in order of knowledge, but that does not mean they are prior in the order of being.' Simons offers an analysis of substance in terms of 'trope bundles' (bundles of *property instances*), one which has found favour in some quarters of late. Lowe, in his paper, argues against such an analysis.

The theme of this collection is Aristotelian metaphysics; but since, for the Aristotelian, metaphysics is as it were the engine that drives every other field of philosophy, it is interesting and important to see an example of how this works in practice. John Haldane provides just such an illustration, by demonstrating the relevance of form and matter to the philosophy of mind. A proper understanding of this central area of current debate sees it as really about the *metaphysics* of mind: what is the structure of the mind and its interactions with the world? How does this help to explain thought, action and personhood, the three large topics which Haldane points out are at the core of the philosophy of mind? After surveying the present state of the debate and pointing out in particular the predominant *physicalism, reductionism* and *naturalism* which characterize most current theories, Haldane goes on to argue that an account of the concept of form and of its application to the mind and its operations suggests the possibility of a more satisfactory theory, one which avoids the various forms of naturalistic reductionism and offers a unified account of the person.

Kit Fine has a different concern, namely the question of *mixture*. Mixture is central to Aristotle's thinking, because 'every concrete substance is composed of mixtures and underlying every substantial change is a process of mixing.' Hence to understand substance and substantial change we need to understand mixtures and mixing. Drawing on Aristotle's own account and on recent work including his own detailed and important study, Fine offers an overview of the problem as well as his own theory in terms of form and disposition.

A distinctive feature of Aristotelianism is the central role of biology in metaphysics. It would be going too far to suggest, as some have, that metaphysics is really the 'handmaiden of biology'; nevertheless we cannot understand the whole of reality without understanding biology, because life is one of its key elements, in many ways its most important and perhaps most mysterious. Again Aristotelianism can be seen as a corrective to the prevailing *physicalism* of modern philosophy, which seeks to explain all of reality in terms of the fundamental concepts of physics. This is no part of Aristotle's thought, since for him biology is an independent and irreducible science in its own right. Joshua Hoffman and Gary Rosenkrantz, who have done important recent work on substance, take biology every bit as seriously as Aristotle, and attempt to give a complete theory of organic life. They do so by showing how the analysis of what it is to be a living thing differs radically from the analysis of non-living compounds. These latter are to be analyzed in terms of the notion of an equilibrium of attractive and repulsive forces, whereas life must be explained in terms of functional connectedness, control and regulation. Their paper shows what such an account might look like.

Finally, Michael Rea tackles one of the most hotly debated problems in contemporary metaphysics, that of *material constitution*. What is it for one thing to constitute another, say a lump of bronze and a statue? The statue and the lump seem to share all their parts, which tempts us to say they are really one and the same object. And yet things are true of the statue which are not true of the bronze: the former cannot survive being melted down or having its parts radically rearranged, whereas the latter can. This inclines us to say they are distinct objects. So which is true? Rea outlines the solutions which have been canvassed, and says we should look closely at a variation on the idea that the statue and the lump are not identical, one which does not, however, entail that the lump and the statue are *two* objects in the same place at the same time. Rea claims that this view, exploiting the idea of *numerical sameness without identity*, can be derived from Aristotle's own thought about 'accidental sameness'. Whilst not denying the difficulties inherent in this proposed solution, Rea argues that it should be taken seriously as a way through the vexing problem of constitution.

This collection grew out the fourth annual *Ratio* conference held at the University of Reading in April 1997. The editor would like to thank Jonathan Lowe, Peter Simons and John Haldane, who presented papers, as well as Kit Fine, Joshua Hoffman and Gary Rosenkrantz, and Michael Rea, who kindly agreed to provide written contributions. Thanks are also due to the Mind Association and the Analysis Committee, which gave financial support to the conference, to all those at the University of Reading who helped to organize it, and to Keith Horton for his valuable editorial assistance.

David S. Oderberg
Associate Editor, RATIO
d.s.oderberg@reading.ac.uk

I

FORM WITHOUT MATTER

E. J. Lowe

Abstract
Three different concepts of matter are identified: matter as what a thing is immediately made of, matter as stuff of a certain kind, and matter in the (dubious) sense of material 'substratum'. The doctrine of hylomorphism, which regards every individual concrete thing as being 'combination' of matter and form, is challenged. Instead it is urged that we do well to *identify* an individual concrete thing with its own particular 'substantial form'. The notions of form and matter, far from being correlative, are relatively independent. There is nothing absurd in the notion of *form without matter*. Matter provides neither a principle of individuation nor a criterion of identity for individual concrete things: their form alone provides both. Finally, a substance ontology which admits also the existence of particular qualities, or tropes, is to be preferred both to a substance ontology which denies the existence of tropes and to a pure trope ontology.

According to some Aristotle scholars, Aristotle changed doctrine concerning primary substance between composing the *Categories* and composing the *Metaphysics*. By this account, the primary substances of the *Categories* are individual concrete objects or things, such as a particular horse or a particular house, whereas in the *Metaphysics* such things are deemed to be combinations of matter and substantial form and as such not themselves primary substances, the status of primary substance now being assigned to substantial forms.[1] This supposed change of doctrine is sometimes put down to the need to provide a satisfactory account of *change*, one that is consistent with the belief that nothing is ever either created from nothing or wholly annihilated. I have no intention to get involved with questions of Aristotelian exegesis here, though I do want to defend the doctrine of the *Categories*,

---

[1] See, e.g., Alan Code, 'Aristotle: Essence and Accident', in R. E. Grandy & R. Warner (eds.), *Philosophical Grounds of Rationality* (Oxford: Clarendon Press, 1986) and Michael Frede, 'Substance in Aristotle's *Metaphysics*', in his *Essays in Ancient Philosophy* (Oxford: Clarendon Press, 1987).

whether or not Aristotle himself later abandoned or modified it. But I also want to argue that, in a perfectly good sense, it is possible to assign the status of primary substance *both* to individual concrete objects *and* to substantial forms – because it is possible to identify items of these types. This may seem inconsistent with the idea that individual concrete objects are combinations of matter and substantial form – the theory of hylomorphism – and, indeed, it is so, at least if we understand the term 'combination' in this context as expressing a relation between parts of a whole. But such an understanding needs to be rejected, as we shall see when we come to discuss the notion of matter. Another problem might be thought to be that substantial forms are universals rather than particulars and hence not identifiable with individual concrete things of any kind. To this I reply that I am thinking now of *individual* substantial forms, rather than of the universals which such individuals instantiate. However, all of this will, I hope, become clear in what follows.

Let us examine now the concept – or, more exactly, the concepts – of matter. There are at least three different concepts of matter with which we must deal, though these concepts may overlap in their extensions. All of the concepts are implicit in Aristotle's own writings, though, once more, I am not concerned here with the niceties of Aristotle scholarship. First, there is the concept of proximate matter, which is a relative notion: it is the concept of *what a thing is immediately made of.* This is a relative notion inasmuch as x may be immediately made of y and y may be immediately made of z, in which case x is made of z, though z is not x's *proximate* matter, because x is not *immediately* made of z. Of course, x may – and usually will – be immediately made of a plurality of items, as when a heap of sand is immediately made of many grains, so that our variables 'x', 'y' and 'z' here should be interpreted as having pluralities of items as well as single items as their possible values.

Our second concept of matter is the notion of a *kind of stuff,* that is, a kind of space-filling material which has separable parts capable of filling different parts of space. Matter in this sense may be either *homoeomerous* or *heteromerous,* that is, it may either be made of uniform parts of the same kind throughout its extension or else it may be made, at some level of composition, of parts of a different kind. For example, gold, we now believe, is a heteromerous stuff, because it is made of gold atoms and these are not made of yet smaller golden parts but rather of protons, neutrons and electrons. But even if no homoeomerous stuffs actually exist, they could have done: gold would have been a homoeomerous stuff if every part of it had been made of smaller golden parts, *ad infinitum*. Clearly, our first concept of matter may overlap in its extension with our second concept of matter: what something is immediately made of may be stuff of a certain kind. Actual examples are not hard to think of. Thus, an individual rubber ball is immediately made of rubber: that is, a part or portion of rubber is the proximate matter of the ball. My own view, I should explain, is that the ball is not to be *identified* with the part of rubber of which it is made, since these items very probably differ in their histories and certainly differ in their modal properties. (The part of rubber may have been synthesised before being formed into a spherical shape to create the ball; and, certainly, the part of rubber could continue to exist even if the ball were to be destroyed – for instance, if the part of rubber were to be divided into many separate pieces.) Thus, on my view, *composition is not identity*. I shall return to this claim later and defend it against a certain kind of objection.

Our third concept of matter is the notion of *material substratum*. This is the notion of an item which provides ontological support for a thing's properties – the notion of that in which a thing's properties 'inhere'. One thought behind this notion is the thought that the properties of a thing are ontologically dependent entities, which cannot exist separately from that thing. Here, it would seem, properties are themselves being thought of as *particulars*, that is, as what used to be called 'individual accidents' but are now more commonly referred to as 'tropes'.[2] My own preferred term for such items, which also has venerable precedent, is 'modes'. The thought, then, is that because modes are ontologically dependent entities, they must depend for their existence upon items of a *different* type – and material substrata are invoked as the items filling this role. Various objections may, of course, be raised against this doctrine. Most obviously, it may be objected that material substrata would have themselves to be quite featureless, lacking properties of their own while 'supporting' the properties of the things whose substrata they were. The reasoning behind this objection is that if material substrata were allowed to have properties of their own,

---

[2] On tropes, see Keith Campbell, *Abstract Particulars* (Oxford: Blackwell, 1990).

then they would stand in need of material substrata themselves in support of those properties and thus a regress would be initiated, which could only be terminated either by propertyless substrata or else by substrata whose properties stood in need of no support. But if there could be substrata with properties standing in need of no support, then the motivation for introducing substrata in the first place would have been undermined, so that the substratum theory is committed to the existence of propertyless substrata in order to avoid an infinite regress which would certainly appear to be vicious.

However, the foregoing objection to substratum theory is certainly open to challenge. Remember, I introduced the notion of material substratum as the notion of an item which provides ontological support for a thing's properties. But why shouldn't we say that it is *the thing itself* – the thing which *has* the properties – which provides ontological support for those properties and which thus occupies the role of 'material substratum'? If we say this, then we are by no means committed, of course, to saying that material substrata are themselves featureless. But if we do say this, we must certainly also say that things and their properties – in the sense of their modes or individual accidents – are items belonging to quite different ontological categories, since the former are now being conceived of as being ontologically independent entities in contrast with the latter: in short, the former – the things which have the properties – are being conceived of as *individual substances.* That is precisely what I, following the Aristotle of the *Categories*, do want to say, of course. But I concede that I must earn the right to do so. Suffice it for now to say, however, that the objection to the notion of material substratum raised earlier only damages a particular version of the substratum theory.

There is another way in which some philosophers react to the objection raised earlier to the notion of material substratum. These philosophers concede that properties – or, as they prefer to call them, tropes – are ontologically dependent entities, but do not accept that this implies that they must depend for their existence upon items of a quite different type, material substrata or individual substances. They contend that tropes merely depend for their existence *upon each other*, holding at the same time that certain bundles or aggregates of interdependent tropes enjoy a kind of ontological independence, inasmuch as the members of such a trope-bundle do not depend for their existence upon any items outside the bundle.[3] According to this view, the items that we call individual concrete things – such as an individual apple or chair – are precisely such trope-bundles, the implication being that such things are not, after all, properly characterised as 'individual substances', at least if the latter term is intended to designate a type of item belonging to a quite different category from that of the tropes themselves. I shall say more about this view later.

Where have we got to so far? I have identified three different concepts of matter: the concept of proximate matter (what a thing is immediately made of), the concept of a kind of stuff, and the concept of material substratum. I have also suggested that an intelligible – and perhaps the only intelligible – interpretation of the third concept is to treat it as coinciding precisely with the notion of an individual substance, as Aristotle conceived of this in the *Categories*, that is, as coinciding with the notion of an individual concrete thing or object. Again, I have pointed out that the first concept of matter may at least overlap with the second concept, because what a thing is immediately made of may simply be stuff of a certain kind. At the same time, however, it must be acknowledged that, very often, what a thing is immediately made of is *not* stuff of a certain kind, but rather certain other things. For instance, a ship is immediately made of planks and spars and nails and ropes and so forth – and these are not themselves parts of stuff of any kind, though some of them (such as the nails) are indeed immediately made of parts of stuff of certain kinds. Modern science, of course, suggests that every macroscopic thing is *ultimately* made of microscopic things, such as quarks and electrons, rather than of parts of stuff of any kind. It also suggests that things such as quarks and electrons are themselves *not made of anything*, because they are simple or non-composite entities. If that is so, then quarks and electrons provide examples of things which, though clearly 'physical', are wholly 'immaterial', in the sense that they lack proximate matter of any kind. Against this, it might, I suppose, be urged that quarks and electrons are made of 'energy' and thus of a certain kind of stuff. But this would almost certainly seem to involve a serious misconception of the nature of energy.

Next I want to look at the notion of *form*, which in Aristotle's *Metaphysics* seems to be treated as correlative with that of matter

---

[3] See, e.g., Peter Simons, 'Particulars in Particular Clothing: Three Trope Theories of Substance', *Philosophy and Phenomenological Research* 54 (1994), pp. 553–575.

– though again I should issue the warning that I do not wish to engage here in the disputes of rival Aristotle scholars. The doctrine of hylomorphism seems to be that every individual concrete thing is, in some sense, a 'combination' of matter and form. A standard example is that of a bronze statue, whose matter is bronze and whose form (it seems) is a certain shape imposed upon that bronze. Here it appears that it is the notion of *proximate* matter that is being invoked as correlative with the notion of form. Aristotle himself, it seems clear, believed in the existence of homoeomerous stuffs, because he was opposed to atomism. He also seems to have believed that all such stuffs somehow arose from the presence within them, in different proportions or ratios, of the four supposed elements – fire, air, earth and water. This aspect of his doctrine does not now much concern me, interesting though it may be to try to make sense of it.[4] Of equally small concern to me is the question of whether or not someone, like Aristotle, who believes in the existence of homoeomerous stuffs is committed to the existence of so-called 'prime matter' – and indeed the deeper question of whether the notion of prime matter makes sense. I did not identify the notion of prime matter as a fourth concept of matter distinct from any of the previous three, because it is clearly a special case of the concept of matter as stuff of a certain kind (the second concept). At the same time, however, it does seem that some philosophers have been inclined to identify the notion of prime matter with that of material substratum, though only those wedded to the version of the substratum theory which I have rejected, that is, the version according to which material substratum is itself featureless. Indeed, some philosophers seem to suggest, rather darkly, that this supposed identity between prime matter and 'featureless' material substratum might somehow receive support from the idea that prime matter has only 'potential', as opposed to 'actual', existence. However, all such thoughts are too dark for me and I shall consider them no further here. I only want to say that it seems to me perfectly intelligible to suppose, first, that homoeomerous stuffs *might* have existed and, second, that there might have been just *one* fundamental kind of homoeomerous stuff to which all parts of stuff belonged. If the latter had been the case, it would still have been possible for different parts of

    [4]   See, e.g., Kit Fine, 'The Problem of Mixture', in F. A. Lewis & R. Bolton (eds), *Form, Matter, and Mixture in Aristotle* (Oxford: Blackwell, 1996).

stuff to be qualitatively different from one another, but nothing would have warranted our calling this single kind of stuff 'prime matter', if by that is meant a kind of stuff the parts of which supposedly have *no qualities whatever*. For I can make no sense of the idea of such a featureless kind of stuff.

But we must return to the issue of form. The hylomorphic theory, it seems, conceives of a thing's form as the way in which its proximate matter has to be organised or arranged in order for a thing of that kind, made of that matter, to exist. Thus, a piece of bronze has to be shaped in a certain way in order for a statue, made of that bronze, to exist. In what sense, then, if any, is a particular bronze statue a 'combination' of matter and form? Not, I think, in any mereological sense.[5] The piece of bronze composing a statue is not a *part* of the statue. For it could only be a part of the statue if it were either a proper or an improper part of it (an improper part of a whole being a part of it which over-laps every part of it). It is not the latter (an improper part), because then it would be *identical* with the statue, which I have already claimed it is not. Nor, however, is it the former (a proper part), for there is no part of the statue which it fails to overlap. (To concede, thus, that it overlaps every part of the statue is not to concede that it is, after all, an improper part of the statue, because it is not yet to concede that it is a part of the statue at all.) Nor is the form of the statue a part of it, since it is, rather, the way in which the statue's various material parts are organised or arranged (or so we are presently assuming) – and the arrange-ment of certain parts cannot itself be one of those parts, as this would involve the very conception of an arrangement of parts in a fatal kind of impredicativity. Talk, then, of matter and form 'combining' must be explicated in another way if it is to make any sense at all. My own view is that such talk is not, ultimately, very helpful and only tends to lead philosophers astray.

As I have already indicated, it is at least superficially plausible to think of a thing's form, such as the form of a statue, as being a *way* – thus, in the case of the statue, a way in which its proximate matter, the bronze, is shaped. (I should warn, however, that we shall soon see reason to modify this particular judgement concerning the form of the statue, while retaining aspects of the

---

[5] For a contrary view to mine, see Sally Haslanger, 'Parts, Compounds and Substantial Unity', in T. Scaltsas, D. Charles & M. L. Gill (eds), *Unity, Identity and Explanation in Aristotle's Metaphysics* (Oxford: Clarendon Press, 1994).

more general insight that talk of 'ways' provides.) Such a 'way' is nothing other than what I earlier called a *mode*, as indeed the words themselves suggest. So what we are talking about here are particular properties, or property instances. (I shall, for the time being, avoid the terminology of 'tropes'.) These are to be contrasted with *universals*, conceived of as the *types* of which property instances or modes are *tokens*. I myself favour a rather liberal ontology which embraces both universals and particulars, though I shall not undertake to defend that stance just now. For present purposes, my chief focus is on particulars. Now, however, we immediately run into what appears to be a difficulty. I have suggested (though only provisionally) that the 'form' of the statue is the particular way in which the bronze composing it is shaped, and that this particular 'way' is a mode or property instance. But *of what* is it a property – the bronze, or the statue, or both? We are under some pressure to say that the form belongs to the statue *rather than* to the bronze (perhaps because the hylomorphic theory tells us that the statue is a 'combination' of matter and form, that is, of the bronze and a certain shape, though I shall identify a better reason than this shortly). But the bronze and the statue are, while the former composes the latter, exactly the same in shape. Do they, then, have numerically distinct but exactly coinciding shapes, with the shape of the statue being its 'form' while the shape of the bronze is, as some might put it, a mere 'accident' of the bronze? The thought here would be that the statue's shape is essential to it, whereas the bronze's shape is non-essential. However, the notion that two distinct but qualitatively indistinguishable shapes could exactly coincide is highly contentious, raising a host of metaphysical issues. But rather than address those issues just now, I shall return to this question later, when I come to discuss trope theory.

If we are to regard the 'form' of the statue as something belonging exclusively to the statue *rather than* to the bronze, we do well, it seems, to identify that form with a particular property which the statue has but the bronze does not. There is such a property, of course: the property of *being a statue of such-and-such a shape*. Put this way, however, we may seem to be talking of that property as a *universal* rather than a *particular*. After all, many different individual statues, it might be said, can have the property of being a statue of such-and-such a shape. But if we follow my earlier suggestion and acknowledge the existence of properties *both* in the sense of universals *and* in the sense of particulars

– that is, in the sense of particular property instances – then we may want to say that each individual statue has a *particular* property of being a statue of such-and-such a shape, just as it has a particular shape or colour. In fact, though, I suggest that what we *should* say is that each individual statue doesn't *have*, but *is*, a particular instance of the universal '(being a) statue of such-and-such a shape'. This is because I want to distinguish between two different types of universal: *substantial* universals and *non-substantial* universals. In general, the former are denoted by *sortal* terms, such as 'statue' and 'tiger', whereas the latter are denoted by *adjectival* terms, such as 'red' and 'spherical'. The particular instances of non-substantial universals are what I earlier called *modes* – and these are ontologically dependent entities, depending for their existence upon the individual concrete things whose modes they are. The particular instances of substantial universals, however, are just the individual concrete things themselves, such as particular statues and particular tigers. So the position that I am recommending is this. If we want to make sense of the distinction between matter and form – where by 'matter', now, we understand *proximate* matter – then we do well to *identify* an individual concrete thing with its own particular 'substantial form'. This, then, will enable us to accept *both* Aristotle's view of the *Categories* that individual concrete things are the primary substances *and* the view, sometimes attributed to Aristotle on the basis of what he says in the *Metaphysics*, that particular substantial forms are the primary substances. For, according to my suggestion, these two doctrines exactly coincide.

The position we have arrived at implies, of course, that it is not, after all, the particular *shape* of the statue which is its 'form', but rather, as it were, the statue's particular *being a statue of such a shape* – something which, as we have seen, I want simply to identify with *the statue itself*. And, surely, it *must* be the statue's particular *being a statue of such a shape*, rather than just its particular *shape*, which is its 'form', if we take it (as I think we must) that a thing's form determines its identity over time. For the statue's merely having that particular shape does not, as such, constrain its identity over time at all, whereas its being a *statue* of that shape most certainly does.

This is an appropriate place to observe, concerning my claim that *composition is not identity*, that some philosophers find it surprisingly difficult to understand how two different things, with

different persistence conditions – such as the bronze statue and
the piece of bronze composing it – can exist in the same place at
the same time.[6] They point out that these things have exactly the
same components while they coincide – in this case, a certain set
of bronze particles – and they cannot understand how these same
components can simultaneously compose two different objects
with different modal properties, for they assume that the modal
properties of a composite object must supervene upon the properties and relations of its components. (Here it should be noted
that a thing's persistence conditions qualify as modal properties
of that thing, for they determine what kinds of change that thing
can and cannot survive.) However, these philosophers apparently
fail to grasp two vital points. The first is that whether or not a
persisting object of a certain kind exists in a certain place at a
certain time is not in general determined purely by facts concerning what else exists *at that time*, but typically also depends on facts
concerning what else exists *before and after that time* and how those
other things are related *over* time. The second is that it is in virtue
of *different* transtemporal relations between their components
that composite things of different kinds persist through time.
Thus, what is required for a piece of bronze to persist is that the
same bronze particles should remain united together over time,
whereas what is required for a bronze statue to persist is that *some*
(but not necessarily the same) bronze particles should be successively united together so as to preserve the same overall shape.
(These requirements, I should add, are of an a priori character –
and the modal properties associated with them are consequently
quite unlike ordinary dispositional properties, such as solubility:
for instance, those modal properties are not 'grounded', as solubility is commonly thought to be, in categorical properties of a
thing's microstructural constituents.) If one takes, as it were, a
mental snapshot of the bronze statue as it is at a certain moment
of time, then, of course, one will not perceive any discernible
difference between it and the piece of bronze composing it at
that time. But, equally, if one takes a mental snapshot of a *moving*
object at a moment of time, one will not perceive any discernible

⁶ See, e.g., Michael B. Burke, 'Copper Statues and Pieces of Copper', *Analysis* 52
(1992), pp. 12–17, Dean W. Zimmerman, 'Theories of Masses and Problems of
Constitution', *Philosophical Review* 104 (1995), pp. 53–110 and Eric T. Olson,
'Composition and Coincidence', *Pacific Philosophical Quarterly* 77 (1996), pp. 374–403. For
further discussion, see my 'Coinciding Objects: In Defence of the "Standard Account"',
Analysis 55 (1995), pp. 171–8.

difference between it and an otherwise exactly similar stationary object. This just goes to show, unsurprisingly, that statuehood, like motion, is a 'diachronic' property, whose exemplification at a time is underdetermined by purely synchronic facts concerning things existing at that time.

Our current position has some other interesting and, perhaps, genuinely surprising implications. One of these is that, contrary to the doctrine of hylomorphism, the notions of form and matter, far from being correlative, are relatively independent. There is nothing absurd in the notion of *form without matter*. Of course, we have already noted that modern science apparently acknowledges the existence of individual concrete things which are 'matterless', in the sense of having no proximate matter: the fundamental particles of modern physics are not conceived of as being 'made of' (that is, composed of) anything whatever. But, according to the conception of 'form' which I am advocating, this does not constrain us to deny that such particles have *form*. Each such particle may, consistently with what I have said so far, be taken simply to *be* (identical with) a particular 'substantial form'. Thus, a particular electron could be taken simply to be a particular instance of the substantial universal '(being an) electron'. In fact, the only thing which stands in the way of our saying this is that it appears that electrons and other so-called fundamental particles do not possess fully determinate identity conditions, owing to the quantum-mechanical phenomenon of superposition or 'entanglement'.[7] It may be, indeed, that a field interpretation of quantum processes is ultimately preferable to a particle interpretation, in which case we shouldn't think of 'electron' as a sortal term at all. But these are issues which I do not wish to go into here. Suffice it to say that the concept of a matterless individual substance is perfectly coherent, even if physics does not provide us with uncontentious examples of such items.

This idea of individual substances possessing form without matter is not at all novel, of course. Leibnizian monads would seem to fit this description exactly, as would Cartesian souls. (The vulgar notion, propagated by some modern physicalist philosophers, that Cartesian souls are supposed to made of some sort of ghostly, 'immaterial' stuff – a near contradiction in terms – is quite unwarranted.) However, I imagine that these historical

[7]   See further my 'Vague Identity and Quantum Indeterminacy', *Analysis* 54 (1994), pp. 110–14 and my 'Entity, Identity and Unity', *Erkenntnis* (forthcoming).

comparisons may immediately ring alarm bells in some philosophers' minds. In particular, worries may arise concerning the
individuation of entities of the sort we are contemplating. One
venerable tradition – exemplified in the writings of Aquinas – has
it that matter is 'the principle of individuation'. Here the thought
is that all that can be guaranteed to distinguish two different
concrete things of exactly the same kind – two different tigers, say
– is the different matter of which they are composed. Hence,
matterless kinds of things would admit of no principled differen-
tiation into numerically distinct instances of those kinds. Thus, it
seems, Aquinas took the view that angels, being immaterial
beings, could only differ *specifically*, not merely *numerically*, from
one another, which implies that each angel is an *infima species* – a
lowest species – rather than a particular instance of a species.
Leibniz, famously, extended this conclusion to all substances, in
line with his doctrine of the identity of indiscernibles.[8]

On these questions, however, I depart from traditional thinking. (In what follows, I should point out, I shall not distinguish
between matter conceived of as a kind of stuff and matter
conceived of as what a thing is made of, because it seems that
Aquinas and Leibniz themselves were not laying any weight on
this distinction in connection with the issues now under debate.)
First of all, I think it important to distinguish very carefully
between questions of identity and questions of individuation.[9] A
principle of individuation, as I understand that term, is a principle which tells us what is to count as *one* instance of a given kind
– for example, what is to count as one tiger or one ship. A criterion of identity, by contrast, is a principle which tells us what
makes for the identity or diversity of items of a given kind – for
example, what makes for the identity or diversity of this ship with
that ship. As a consequence, it seems to me that matter is
certainly *not* a 'principle of individuation' of individual concrete
things (things like tigers and ships): on the contrary, their *form* is
what 'individuates' such things. For it is the form of a tiger which
determines its status as being a *single* thing of a certain kind, a
unitary whole composed of suitably organized parts. Indeed, one
feature which distinguishes individual concrete things, such as
individual tigers, from mere parts or portions of material stuff is

---

[8] See G. W. Leibniz, *Discourse on Metaphysics* [1686], trans. P. G. Lucas & L. Grint
(Manchester: Manchester University Press, 1953), p. 14.
[9] See further my 'Entity, Identity and Unity'.

that the latter *lack* any distinctive principle of individuation. This is why we cannot *count* parts of material stuff in any principled way – why, for instance, it makes no sense to ask *how many* parts or portions of gold there are in a certain room, but at most only *how much* gold there is there altogether. Parts of material stuff precisely *fail* to have any distinctive form of their own, since such a part can receive any shape whatever and be dispersed into separate bits or gathered together into a lump. Moreover, every part of material stuff (or at least every such part of macroscopic size, in the case of heteromerous stuffs) consists of lesser parts of the same stuff, since every such part is indefinitely divisible in indefinitely many different ways. Parts of material stuff can at best only be individuated derivatively, in relation to individual concrete things which they may happen to compose. For example, a part of gold might be singled out as the gold which currently wholly composes a certain individual gold ring.

Might it then be that matter, rather than being the 'principle of individuation' of individual concrete things, provides a criterion of *identity* for them? Indeed, is not this really what is meant by the doctrine described above as being attributable to Aquinas? The idea, then, is that what makes for the numerical *distinctness* or *diversity* (non-identity) of two different tigers, say, is the numerical distinctness of the matter composing them. But this idea can certainly be challenged, on the simple grounds that individual concrete things like tigers can and do *change* their component matter. Indeed, in principle, two different tigers could, over a period of time, entirely *exchange* their component matter with one another. So the most that can be said is that two different tigers cannot share the same matter *at the same time*. But why not? Simply because that would require the two tigers to exist in exactly the same place at the same time, which we deem to be impossible. However, then it transpires that what really makes for the diversity of our two tigers is their difference in spacetime location, from which their difference in component matter at any time merely follows as a consequence. Moreover, that tigers are differentiated by their spacetime locations is clearly itself a consequence of their *form*, since it has to do with what *kind* of thing they are. (Recall, indeed, my earlier remarks to the effect that it is form which determines a thing's identity over time.) This is brought out by the fact that certain (different) kinds of entity apparently *can* exist in the same place at the same time, such as a rubber ball and the piece of rubber composing it, for this highlights the fact that the mutual exclusion of different tigers from the same place at the same time is simply a consequence of their being things of the *same substantial kind*.[10] I conclude, then, that matter provides neither a principle of individuation nor a criterion of identity for individual concrete things: their form alone provides both. In consequence, there is nothing inherently problematic about the notion of individual concrete things which are 'matterless': that is to say, their lacking matter need in no way compromise either the individuability or the identity of such entities. (This applies, I should say, whether or not we think of 'matter' in this context as a kind of stuff or merely as what something is made of.) This is not to say there are no problems whatever concerning the individuation and identity of such entities, only that there are none which accrue simply from the fact that they are conceived to be 'matterless'.

Another misconception which we should dispose of is the idea that matterless individuals would have to be *extensionless* and so either punctiform or else altogether non-spatial. This idea is based, perhaps, on the thought that any spatially extended object must at least contain spatially distinct parts and consequently, if those parts are to be distinguishable from mere parts of space itself, they must be distinct *material* parts of the object. But this is to confuse the notion of a spatial part of a thing with that of a component or material part of it (in the sense of 'material' which corresponds to the concept of matter as what a thing is made of). Even when a spatially extended thing *does* have material parts, they are never to be *identified* with spatial parts of that thing.[11] For instance, the top half of a rubber ball is not to be identified with the portion of rubber currently occupying that top half, not least because, through a rearrangement of the material of the ball, a *different* portion of rubber could come to occupy that top half. There is no reason why there should not exist a spatially extended individual concrete thing which was not *composed* of anything at all, neither of parts of stuff nor of other individual concrete things (just as an electron is, in this sense, non-composite). In particular, there need be no problem about

---

[10] See further David S. Oderberg, 'Coincidence under a Sortal', *Philosophical Review* 105 (1996), pp. 145–71. I disagree, then, with the claims of Christopher Hughes, 'Same-Kind Coincidence and the Ship of Theseus', *Mind* 106 (1997), pp. 53–67.

[11] See further my 'Primitive Substances', *Philosophy and Phenomenological Research* 54 (1994), pp. 531–52, especially pp. 544–5.

distinguishing such a spatially extended individual from the region of space which it occupies, because it may have *qualities and powers* which that region of space lacks – and while retaining those qualities and powers it may trace a path through space by successively occupying different regions of space. So, once we recognise that a spatially extended thing, although possessing spatial parts, is certainly not *composed* of those parts, even if it is composed of anything at all, we can see that there is nothing problematic about the notion of a non-composite or simple thing which is nonetheless spatially extended.[12] Whether there are any actual examples of such things is a more contentious issue. I hesitate to offer the example of fundamental physical particles, not only because (as remarked earlier) a field interpretation of quantum phenomena may ultimately be preferable to a particle interpretation, but also because, even on a particle interpretation, it is questionable whether such particles can be said to be spatially extended in any very straightforward sense. However, elsewhere I have offered the example of *persons* as very possibly being things which are non-composite and yet which are also (at least when embodied) spatially extended.[13] The thought behind this suggestion is that a person is not *composed* by his or her body, nor by any material parts thereof: the relation of embodiment is, I think, quite different from that of composition. But I shall say no more about this here.

I have, of course, been defending a substance ontology, in which individual concrete things are – as they were for the Aristotle of the *Categories* – the primary substances. My ontology also admits both universals and particulars: substantial universals, whose particular instances are individual concrete things, and non-substantial universals, whose particular instances are *modes* of those individual concrete things. (I should say that I also admit *relations*, both as universals and as particulars, but to avoid unnecessary complication I shall say no more about these here.) Such a four-category ontology may seem extravagant to many metaphysicians, but I think I can justify it. The case for realism about universals does not really concern me just here, though I would base it on the need to explain the status of

---

[12] Here I disagree with Dean W. Zimmerman, 'Could Extended Objects be Made out of Simple Parts? An Argument for "Atomless Gunk"', *Philosophy and Phenomenological Research* 56 (1996), pp. 1–29: see, especially, p.8.

[13] See my *Subjects of Experience* (Cambridge: Cambridge University Press, 1996), pp. 39–44.

natural laws.[14] Of more immediate concern to me now is the question of why we should admit to our ontology, as belonging to irreducibly different categories, both individual substances and their modes. In this respect my ontology has two distinct rivals: on the one hand an ontology which admits, as particulars, only individual substances (what I have hitherto called individual concrete things) and on the other hand an ontology which admits, as particulars, only modes - or, as its adherents commonly prefer to call them, tropes.

Let us first look at the ontology which admits, as particulars, only individual substances. Such an ontology will not find it easy to do without universals, because there are seemingly intractable difficulties besetting any attempt to combine such an ontology with a doctrine of resemblance nominalism. But such an ontology, if it admits universals, cannot make a principled distinction between (what I have called) substantial and non-substantial universals. It cannot distinguish, in any very fundamental way, between saying that an individual substance is a *ball* or a *leaf* and saying that it is *round* or *green*. In both cases, it must represent such a state of affairs as one in which an individual substance instantiates a certain universal. But to me it seems plainly mistaken to say that an individual leaf, say, is an *instance* of the universal green: rather, I should say that the leaf *exemplifies* that universal, but only in the sense that it possesses a particular property or mode which – unlike the leaf itself – *is* an instance of the universal green. However, I do not expect this consideration to weigh very heavily with the devotees of the ontology now under scrutiny – indeed, they may count it a virtue of their position that it accords no special status to substantial kinds.[15] What are they to say, though, about the phenomenology of object-perception? When I see a green leaf, do I not see the very greenness of the leaf, rather than just the leaf itself? To this advocates of the theory may reply that they conceive of universals in an 'Aristotelian' fashion, as existing *in re* or 'immanently', so that greenness (the universal) is, as the popular phrase has it, 'wholly present' in each individual green thing. So, on this view, I *do* see the greenness of the leaf, but what I see is not a *particular* greenness but just the universal, which is 'wholly present' in the leaf (but is also

---

[14] See further my *Kinds of Being: A Study of Individuation, Identity and the Logic of Sortal Terms* (Oxford: Blackwell, 1989), Ch. 8.
[15] See, e.g., D. M. Armstrong, *A World of States of Affairs* (Cambridge: Cambridge University Press, 1997), pp. 65–8.

'wholly present' in other, spatially separate things). But here I protest for the following reason: when I see the leaf *change* in colour – perhaps as it is turned brown by a flame – I seem to see something *cease to exist* in the location of the leaf, namely, its greenness. But it could not be the *universal* greenness which ceases to exist, at least so long as other green things continue to exist. My opponent must say that really what I see is not something ceasing to exist, but merely the leaf's ceasing to instantiate greenness, or greenness ceasing to be 'wholly present' just here. I can only say that that suggestion strikes me as being quite false to the phenomenology of perception. The objects of perception seem, one and all, to be *particulars* – and, indeed, a causal theory of perception (which I myself favour) would appear to require this, since particulars alone seem capable of entering into causal relations.

Let us turn, then, to the trope ontology, which I consider to be a more serious rival to my own. As I remarked earlier, the trope ontologist accepts, in a way, that tropes are ontologically dependent entities, but tries to do without the category of individual substance by arguing that tropes depend on *each other* for their existence, rather than upon substances (conceived as items belonging to a distinct ontological category). What I have been calling 'individual concrete things' and have regarded as being individual substances, the trope ontologist regards as 'bundles' of interdependent and spatiotemporally compresent tropes. As I see it, the most serious problem for the trope ontologist is to provide an adequate account of the *identity*-conditions of tropes, while simultaneously acknowledging their ontologically dependent nature. The trope ontologist is faced, I believe, with a dilemma in this connection, as I shall now try to make clear.

What determines the identity of a trope, such as the redness of a certain red rubber ball? Clearly, the rednesses of two different red rubber balls are numerically distinct rednesses, but what makes them so? One might venture to say that the distinctness of the two rednesses – the two red tropes – is a simple consequence of the distinctness of the two balls to which they respectively belong. This is to invoke the principle that the identity of a trope is determined at least in part by the identity of the thing to which it belongs: in short, it is to say that tropes are *identity-dependent* upon their possessors.[16] However, it is difficult to square this claim

---

[16] On the notion of identity-dependence, see my 'Ontological Dependency', *Philosophical Papers* 23 (1994), pp. 31–48.

with the thesis that the possessors of tropes – the 'things' to which they belong, such a rubber ball – are themselves just bundles of tropes. For, whatever exactly is meant by 'bundle' in this context, it seems clear that a bundle of tropes must in fact be identity-dependent upon the tropes of which it is a bundle. Indeed, only if this is accepted, it seems to me, can the trope ontologist fairly claim to be doing away with an independent ontological category of individual substance. But, pretty clearly, to hold *both* that tropes are identity-dependent upon trope-bundles *and* that trope-bundles are identity-dependent upon their constituent tropes is to fall into a fatal circularity which deprives both tropes and trope-bundles of well-defined identity-conditions altogether.

Evidently, then, the trope theorist must deny that tropes are identity-dependent upon their possessors. But now the theorist needs to explain in what sense tropes are really ontologically dependent entities – why it is, for instance, that a certain trope cannot 'float free' of the trope-bundle to which it belongs and migrate to another bundle. The identity-dependence of a trope upon its possessor would certainly seem to be capable of explaining this, but we have already seen that the trope theorist cannot appeal to any such dependence, given that the possessors of tropes are conceived of as being mere trope-bundles. The trope theorist may indeed urge that certain *kinds* of tropes cannot exist save in combination with those of certain other *kinds* – for instance, that wherever a colour trope exists, it must exist in combination with (that is, be 'compresent' with) a shape trope. The theorist may contend that such necessities derive from fundamental natural laws governing the existence of tropes and thereby hope to explain why it is, for example, that we never encounter a 'free-floating' red trope. Perhaps, in this respect, tropes are rather like the quarks of the standard model of particle physics. (Quarks can apparently only exist in combinations of two or three within other composite particles, such as protons, never on their own – though some attempts to detect 'free' quarks have been made.) However, none of this delivers the consequence that the redness of a particular red rubber ball cannot survive the demise of that ball or migrate to another thing altogether: it would seem to be perfectly free to do so, so long as it is always accompanied by other tropes of suitable kinds. And yet the suggestion that this might happen seems manifestly absurd.

Another difficulty is this: if tropes are not identity-dependent upon their possessors, what *does* determine their identity or diversity? Perhaps it will be suggested that their spacetime location determines this, but this immediately raises a problem, since tropes are supposed to be capable of existing 'compresently' with other tropes – that is, in the *same* spacetime location. To this it might be replied that tropes only exclude other tropes *of the same kind* from their spacetime location, so that two distinct rednesses or roundnesses cannot exactly coincide. But why not? Indeed, it would seem that there are examples which invite the trope theorist to say that two tropes of the same kind *can* exactly coincide. For instance, what is one to say about the roundness tropes of a round ball and a round cavity which it exactly fits? Suppose the round ball fits snugly into a cavity in a piece of plaster which has been moulded around the ball. Both the ball and the piece of plaster are, according to the trope-theorist, trope-bundles, each of which contains a roundness trope. Do they contain the *same* roundness trope, however, or do they contain numerically distinct but exactly similar and coinciding roundness tropes? I think that the trope theorist had better say that they contain numerically distinct roundness tropes, since either the ball or the piece of plaster can be destroyed while leaving the other completely intact. Other examples like this are not difficult to think of. (We met one earlier, when we discussed the case of the shape of the bronze statue and the exactly similar shape of the bronze composing the statue.) But the implication of such examples is that the trope theorist had better not say that tropes exclude other tropes of the same kind from their spacetime location and consequently must concede that trope-identity has to be determined in some other way. But no other way seems available.

Nor can the trope theorist afford to say that it simply doesn't matter how trope identity is determined, or even whether tropes *have* determinate identity at all – though it is open to *me* to say this about 'modes', at least in some instances.[17] For if the possessors of tropes – things like rubber balls and leaves – are just trope-bundles, then *their* identity will depend upon the identity of the tropes they contain, as we have already noted: and the trope theorist cannot afford to say that the identity of such items is itself a matter of no consequence. I simply do not see a way out of this problem for the trope theorist. By contrast, the substance

---

[17] I raise doubts about the determinacy of trope-identity in my 'Ontological Categories and Natural Kinds', *Philosophical Papers* 26 (1997), pp. 29–46 and also in my 'Entity, Identity and Unity'.

ontology is relatively problem-free. According to this ontology, individual concrete things, such as rubber balls and leaves, are deemed to be individual substances and as such ontologically independent entities. The identity-conditions of individual substances are determined by their form and so differ for substances of different substantial kinds. There is no reason, then, either to expect or to demand a uniform account of the identity-conditions of all individual substances: rather, we must proceed on a case-by-case basis. As for modes – as I call particular properties, in preference to calling them tropes – these are conceived as being particular 'ways' individual substances are, such as the particular way in which a ball is shaped or coloured. Thus understood, the ontological dependence of modes upon the substances which possess them is immediately apparent. Modes aren't 'things' or 'objects' which are somehow related to substances, let alone items of which other items, such as rubber balls, are composed. Rather, to speak of a mode of a substance is just to speak of *how* that substance is, in a certain respect. Another way to put this is to say that modes are 'adjectival' upon substances. Consequently, any talk of modes 'migrating' from one substance to another can be seen as involving an absurd category mistake, whereby modes are treated as if they were quasi-substances in their own right. By the same token, the trope theorist's thesis that things such as rubber balls and leaves are 'bundles' of tropes can be seen as involving a confusion between properties and parts. A particular redness is not a *part* of a red rubber ball, as the trope theorist would have it – not even a 'dependent part' – but is, rather, something *predicable* of the ball.

To conclude: I have defended a particular kind of substance ontology, one which is consonant with Aristotle's doctrine in the *Categories* but also consistent with certain aspects of his doctrine in the *Metaphysics*. I reject, however, the doctrine of hylomorphism (understood as implying that every individual concrete thing is a combination of matter and form) as well as the doctrines of 'prime matter' and material substratum, the latter at least in that version of it which sees material substratum as a featureless entity distinct from the thing whose properties it 'supports'. An important aspect of my position is my identification of individual substances with instances of substantial universals, which can be seen as tantamount to identifying an individual substance with a particular 'substantial form'. According to this view of substantial form, the notion of form is not inseparably linked to the notion of matter, neither to the notion of matter as a kind of stuff nor to the notion of matter as what a thing is made of. Consequently, it makes perfect sense on this view to contemplate the possibility of there being 'matterless' substances – form without matter – a possibility which may actually be realised in the case of the fundamental particles of physics and even in the case of individual persons, that is, *ourselves*.

Department of Philosophy
University of Durham
50 Old Elvet
Durham DH1 3HN
UK
e.j.lowe@durham.ac.uk

II

FAREWELL TO SUBSTANCE:
A DIFFERENTIATED LEAVE-TAKING

Peter M. Simons

Abstract
For most of the history of metaphysics, the subject has been domi-
nated by the concept of substance. There is an everyday commonsense notion of substance which is perfectly harmless and which I
shall defend against attempts to remove it or revise it away. But I
deny that substance has to be construed as a primitive even in
everyday terms. Borrowing Strawson's distinction between descriptive and revisionary metaphysics, I press the legitimate claims of
revisionary metaphysics and argue that there is no place for a
fundamental concept of substance within it, although aspects of
the concept are likely to find their place therein.

There are several senses in which a thing is said to be first; yet
substance is first in every sense – (1) in definition; (2) in order
of knowledge; (3) in time.

Aristotle, Metaphysics 1028a30

1 Strands of Substance

The idea of substance was introduced by Aristotle as part of his
critique of Plato's theory of forms and is at the core of his metaphysics. But Aristotle uses the word in two distinct senses, which
apparently reflects a development in his thinking. The first sense
is found in the *Categories*, where Aristotle distinguishes substance
from the other nine categories. Examples of substance in the
primary sense are an individual man, an individual horse. In a
secondary sense the kinds to which these examples belong are
also called substance, but I shall ignore this use. In the *Metaphysics*
however, substance is identified not as the concrete individual,
which is now analysed as the compound of matter and form, but
as the form of the concrete individual, what the medievals called
substantial form. This is prior to the compound, which presupposes it, and prior to the matter it informs, which exists only
potentially, as informed, and which in any case is lent unity and
individuality by the form. There are also passages in Aristotle

suggesting that substantial forms may subsist without matter, in the case of disembodied intelligences responsible for heavenly motion. The complexities of Aristotle's notions and the subsequent modifications the idea of substance received at the hands of the rationalists make it impossible to speak of a single unitary concept of substance in Western philosophy. Rather there are several strands to the concept and I shall unweave some of them relevant to my purpose.

1.1 Independent Beings

The ontological primacy of substances arises chiefly from their independence, or ability to subsist alone. In this they contrast with beings needing others for their existence, such as states, properties or boundaries. But what is meant by 'independent'? There are several senses. A particular object A is *weakly dependent* on another particular B when necessarily, if A exists, so does B. An object is then independent in the corresponding sense when it depends on no particular object (except itself). Objects with essential individual parts, such as the protons of an atom, are dependent in this sense on their essential parts. An object A is *strongly dependent* on an object B if necessarily, if A exists, so does B, and B is neither A nor part of A. When a cat grins, that grin could not exist without that cat, but the cat is not part of the grin, so the grin is strongly dependent on the cat. An object is independent in the corresponding sense when it depends on nothing apart from itself and perhaps parts of itself, giving a sense to the idea of something depending on nothing 'outside itself'. But there are also weaker generic senses of dependence, when an object A depends not on some particular object, but nevertheless could not exist unless there were some object or objects of a certain kind related to it in a certain way. A dog cannot exist without there being a large number of carbon atoms, but which particular carbon atoms go to make up the organic compounds in the dog's body and its food is indifferent.

Qualities, states, actions of a physical body or an organism are all strongly dependent on it; it may be weakly dependent on some essential part, and generically dependent on certain kinds of things, but it is not strongly dependent on any other individual. This allows individuals to have causes – on Aristotle's meaning – yet still be appropriately independent. If having a cause is taken (as in Spinoza) as a form of dependence, then only something uncaused or self-caused can be a substance.

1.2 Ultimate Subjects

Substances are sometimes characterized as the ultimate subjects of predication: that of which things can be predicated but which cannot be predicated of anything else. But this really only defines particulars. What can be predicated (rightly or wrongly) of something is a universal. Dependent particulars such as headaches are not substances. However if we replace 'predication' in the formula by 'inherence', we have the classical account of substances as substrata. A substance is something in which characteristics inhere but which does not itself inhere in anything. Inherence is then a form of dependence under which substances are independent. But if substrata must have characteristics, they are also dependent, though in a different sense: a substratum, while it does not inhere, cannot exist without some characteristics: a 'free substratum' cannot exist.

1.3 Individuators

Where a concrete thing's properties are shareable or universal, the substratum is also that which individuates: a collection of universal properties, no matter how extensive, cannot be immune to being realized twice, so some further, individuating ingredient is required in a concrete particular. Several candidates have been put forward for this role: Aristotelian prime matter is one, place in space is another, Gustav Bergmann's 'bare particulars' are another, like prime matter in being without essential characters, but unlike matter having a pure individuality: they are merely and irreducibly numerically different, and impose this difference on the substances they individuate. A bare particular differs from Duns Scotus's 'thisness' or *haecceitas* in that the thisness of Socrates is not only that which makes the common human nature to be an individual human being: it makes him this particular human being and no other.

1.4 Survivors of Change

Concrete particulars not only have attributes (universal or particular, according to one's theory); they undergo real change. A piece of iron heated in a furnace gets hot, expands, begins to glow, and becomes softer and more malleable. It is widely held that real change consists in this casting off old attributes for new. For something to change, it must exist before, during, and after the change, and so must survive it. Only so can we say it changes, rather than that it was created, replaced by something else, or destroyed. The subjects of change thus 'outlive' whatever ceased to be at the change (the state or accident of the substance), whatever exists fleetingly during it, and pre-exist whatever comes into being at its completion. Concrete particulars also come into being and cease to exist. In familiar cases, they do so by the composition and decomposition of complex structures, or by the arising and subsiding of sustaining processes. Both of these facts suggest there might be more subtle survivors of the demise of substances, such as the matter of which they are made. If substance is primarily that which survives change, then the ultimate substance would be indestructible, whether Aristotle's matter, which never ceases to exist but is merely transformed, or the indestructible, sempiternal atoms of Democritus, or the conserved mass-energy of physics.

1.5 Basic Objects of Reference

Aristotle's *Categories* theory of substances as concrete individuals dovetails less with physical and metaphysical than with linguistic and epistemological concerns. Material things, organisms, geographical features and heavenly bodies are our constant companions through life. We are born of them, marry them, make them, change them, destroy them, buy and sell them, explore them. We fill our waking and sleeping hours talking and thinking about them. Piaget's psychogenetic studies and Strawson's transcendental arguments suggest we could not communicate or even think were we not able to manipulate them, identify, trace and reidentify them. For this to be possible, they must be discriminated by us into sorts, and each sortal concept must connote conditions of persistence and reidentification. To achieve this is, in Quine's words, to learn to divide reference,[1] mastery of which affords us the formal concept of individual and sets us on the road to understanding number. It is the key to further cognitive achievements such as comparing, locating in space and time, describing experiences; it leads us into other ontological categories: quality, amount, position, relation, situation etc., and, via the device of nominalization, making all of these subjects of further predication. If concrete particulars are not the first thing experience as such shows us, they yet seem to be our passport to higher cognition. That they should coincide with the substances of Aristotle's *Categories* is no happenstance:

---

[1] Quine (1960), Section 19.

Aristotle's work is about the meanings of the simple terms we use, so those persistent objects which are so important to our practice of using words were bound to have a salient role in the theory.

2 Everyday Substance Defended

Everyday substances are what we call things or objects, as distinct from their qualities, the relations they stand in to others, the states they have, the events they enter into, the processes in which they are involved. To make clear what everyday substances are we invariably use examples, just as Aristotle did. Of the roles substance is said to carry in the previous section, the most obviously applicable to everyday substances is that they are survivors of change. In recent years the ability of substances to fulfil this role has been challenged. Change, it is said, cannot be adequately explained by invoking substances, because these are three-dimensional objects enduring through time, what C.D. Broad called *continuants*.[2] Therefore they should be construed as or replaced by objects with temporal parts, what Broad called *occurrents*.[3] If this is argument is right, then everyday talk and Western metaphysics from Aristotle to Strawson has been fundamentally wrong about a large proportion of the objects there are in the world. There might be continuants other than substances, but the attack on them is primarily an attack on substances, which everyone can agree are the paradigm examples of continuants.

There are two positions in consideration here, which are not always clearly distinguished. Call them the *replacement position* and the *reconstrual position* respectively. The replacement position is that because continuants are metaphysically deficient, talk about them is to be replaced by talk about suitable occurrents. Thus talk about coffee cups, cats and comets should for metaphysical purposes be replaced by talk about coffee cup processes, cat processes, comet processes, where a coffee cup process is precisely not defined as the process of or history of a coffee cup, but as the kind of process, whatever it is, which leads the person in the street to talk about coffee cups. The metaphysical propriety of such replacement is an interesting and I think open question. If Strawson is right, then there are strong epistemological reasons why we should be unable to carry out such a programme,

---

[2] Broad (1933), pp.138 ff.
[3] Ibid.

because in order to be able to speak a language of subject and predicate we need stable, reidentifiable subjects. I am unconvinced. Quine describes a sequence of language acquisition and theoretic replacement in which we move from feature-placing mass terms to reidentifiable individuals as posits, and then for scientific reasons reconstrue these as four-dimensional processes. Why could we not miss out the middle stage? Or if not us, then an intelligent life-form not so preoccupied with mesoscopic dry individuals. If the metaphysical deficiency of continuants falls short of incoherence, then replacement processes and the continuants they replace could coexist and we could raise the question as to their relationship. The difficulty of the replacement position is that we should need to find ways systematically to develop a vocabulary apt for describing the replacement processes. We should not wish the replacement ontology to be weaker in expressive power than the one it replaced, and the idea that either the same predicates that we already use or some trivial syntactic modification of them will automatically serve up a rich enough vocabulary remains in my view an hypothesis completely untested in detail as it should be if it is to be made credible.

Many opponents of continuants however claim that they are in fact already occurrents, and that a widespread misapprehension prevents blinkered philosophers (and ordinary people perhaps?) from realising this fact. This is the reconstrual position: it is in fact claimed that the reconstrual is the 'proper' construal. Thus David Lewis claims that human beings have temporal parts,[4] and that a human being lasts for a certain number of years, has a temporal extent as well as a spatial extent.

Whichever of these positions is adopted, the chief argument against continuants is that it is impossible to explain properly what intrinsic change consists in.[5] For the advocate of continuants, a change in a continuant consists in a continuant's being first in one way and then in another. If you like properties, you can say that the object has one property at one time and the same object has a contrary property at a later time. If you like tropes, you can say that the object has a trope of one kind at one time and this is replaced by a trope of a contrary kind inhering in the same object at a later time. This is simply what change consists in

---

[4] Lewis (1983), pp.76 ff.
[5] Lewis (1986), pp.202–4.

for continuants. A four-dimensional account of change replaces this view with different properties' being borne by different temporal parts of one and the same extended process. But this is not change but mere temporal diversity, in the same way that a French tricouleur's having a red, a white and a blue part is spatial diversity. It is not change in the standard acceptation because the objects having the contrary properties, the temporal parts, do not survive the change.

It is said that expressions like 'John at 12:45 on 26 April 1997' stand for such temporal parts of the whole process bearing the name 'John'. This misparses sentences in which such strings might occur. If John is unhappy at 10:00 on 25 April 1997 and John is happy at 12:45 on 26 April 1997 then it is *John* who is first unhappy (at the earlier time) and then happy (at the later), not two objects related by genidentity, John-at-10:00-on-25-April-1997 and John-at-12:45-on-26-April-1997, that are respectively unhappy and happy.

The proponents of the four-dimensional view claim that the three-dimensionalist cannot make sense of the idea that the continuant is present as a whole at any time at which it exists. The expression 'present as a whole' gets its force by contrast with the case where at any time an extended occurrent is present only in virtue of the fact that a proper part exists solely at that time. For a continuant to be present or, better, simply to exist at a time, is not for some temporal phase or slice of it to exist and thereby some more compendious whole, but simply for it itself to exist then. A temporal part of an object O over an interval I is an object O_I which is a part of O, which exists at every time in I that O exists, which exists at no times outside I, and which is such that every part of O existing at any time within I is part of it. Occurrents have temporal parts for each interval over which they exist. For them such expressions as 'the part of the football match between 11:00 and 11:15' make sense, and if that part of the football match is exciting then the football match is at least partly exciting. But an individual football player, while he has a life which includes what he does and undergoes between 11:00 and 11:15, does not have a fifteen-minute slice. Rather he is that to which all these things happen: he changes, but does not leave temporal parts behind him as time advances.

It is said that a defence of continuants entails thinking of time in terms of McTaggart's A-series, as consisting of a real past, present and future, whereas the four-dimensionalist can use the more plausible B-series conception of time as untensed, a series ordered by tenseless relations of earlier and later. But while it may be true that our thinking of time in terms of the relation to experienced and so temporally local events may have some general epistemological connection with our thinking of stable configurations around us as continuants, metaphysically there is no necessity for a continuant theorist to embrace A-time. The proof is that one can define and defend continuants while using only B-series talk.[6]

It is said that the relativity of simultaneity makes it impossible to talk about continuants because 'at a time' has no absolute meaning. The defender of continuants does not need to claim that it does. The difference that relativity makes to talk of continuants is that there is no longer an absolute fact of the matter about what parts and properties a large continuant has at a time, because what counts as the same time (for having parts or properties at different places of its extent) varies with frame of reference. That does not mean that what is a spatial part in one frame is a temporal part in another. Any object having parts with spacelike separation in one frame will have parts in spacelike separation in any other frame.

My conclusion is that attempts to shoulder aside the notion of a continuant everyday substance perduring through time fail. The notion is entrenched in our ordinary everyday way of thinking and speaking and it would require a conceptual revolution of unprecedented magnitude to remove or replace it. The motives of those wishing to proclaim its demise are legitimate: they are those of conceptual clarity and conformity to scientific progress. The motives are honourable, but their target is misplaced. The ordinary everyday notion of a continuant individual substance is in its own humble terms all right as it is. This is not to say that difficulties cannot arise. Precisely because it is an everyday notion, and so subject to vagueness and open texture in many cases, it may lead us into difficulty. The familiar problems of identity over time and the reidentification of individuals, in the case of persons and of artifacts like Theseus's Ship make this plain. The attacks on humble substance make the error of supposing the notion is fit to be tidied up and re-presented as belonging to fundamental metaphysics.

[6] Simons (1987), ch. 5.

3 Primitivity of Everyday Substance Contested

If everyday substance is defensible within its own terms, is it a
primitive, unanalysable concept? I think not. I consider that the
most promising account of everyday substance in its role as an
independent being analyses substances as bundles of tropes.[7]
This accords metaphysical priority to tropes and the formal relations which bind them together. Clearly the theory takes its place
within an acceptance of tropes as promising to offer our overall
best account of resemblance. With no universal properties and
relations to require individuation and unification, there is no
need to postulate an individuating substratum, a bare particular
or portion of prime matter. The remaining difficulty is that of
explaining the unity and relative independence of substances. To
overcome the difficulties of both excessive essentialism and
excessive anti-essentialism I proposed a two-tier theory of trope
bundles, whereby a nucleus of tropes, each of which is necessary
to all of the others, constitutes an individual essence while accidental characteristics are catered for by a peripheral halo of
tropes which may be exchanged. The theory is flexible in allowing the extreme cases of bundles without nuclei and also bundles
without halos. The relationships tying bundles together are not,
as in most trope bundle theories, spatial or spatiotemporal comp-
resence. These relations are too weak to engender union where
distinct bundles can interpenetrate and they demand excessive
togetherness where a bundle may be widely spread, as when a
quantum coupled particle pair is formed and the particles fly
apart. The binding relations, which are formal, not themselves
further tropes and so do not engender a regress, are those of existential dependence as defined above, whether mutual or one-
sided, whether rigid or generic. The tropes in a nucleus are
bound by rigid dependence, those in the halo are rigidly dependent on their nucleus but the nucleus requires them, if at all, only
generically.

The relative independence of substances may seem hard to
explain: after all, how can something independent and substantial arise from ethereal, dependent tropes? But if a whole is
composed of a collection of parts each of which has its existential
needs (of whatever strength) met within the collection, then the
collection and therewith the whole it composes requires nothing

---

[7] Simons (1994).

outside it, and is thereby independent. This principle can be used to argue plausibly, following Bolzano, that if there is anything at all, then there is at least one existentially independent thing.[8]

Tropes are standardly invoked to explain how individuals are. They are the truth-makers for atomic predications. If electron Emma is negatively charged, this is because one of her tropes is a negative electric charge trope, distinct from her mass trope and any others she might have. As fulfilling this role, they are best considered to be sparse in relation to logically possible predicates. Not every linguistic predicate corresponds to a trope kind. There are no tropes of existence or self-identity, for example, and many predications will be made true not by a kind of trope corresponding one-to-one with the predicate but by more complex arrangements involving tropes in relation or a whole range of different kinds.

Everyday substances will however be more than just a single trope bundle. Everyday material objects have smaller material objects as their material parts: a human being has limbs, organs, tissues, cells, etc. as parts, and all of these interacting parts are themselves substances and there are tropes, unary and relational, linking and characterising them. A human being is at any one time a hugely complex whole of interrelated parts in static and dynamic relations to one another: most predications are true of such complex wholes because of how the parts are and how they are related. Our shape, size, weight, density etc. derive from the properties of our parts and that they are our parts. Only objects without parts in the common or garden sense are pure bundles of tropes and nothing else. Everything else is a whole of parts which are wholes of parts which are... etc. until we come to the parts which are as they are not because they have parts but because they are bundles of tropes. How larger things are may or may not be determined by how their ultimate parts are and are related; the occurrence of holistic or Gestalt quality tropes dependent on larger wholes is not ruled out, nor is the emergence of tropes unpredictable from the properties of their bearers' parts.

The intricacies and flexibility of this picture are appealing, but it has been claimed by Hoffman and Rosenkrantz that the theory is both inconsistent and inadequate.[9] It is inadequate because it does not allow the possibility of unextended souls as substances.

---

[8]   Simons and Ganthaler (1987), Simons (1987), pp.321–3.
[9]   Hoffman and Rosenkrantz (1994), pp.77 ff.

Hoffman and Rosenkrantz's criticisms include several that are misplaced because they do not faithfully represent my theory. Among these are that there could be no trope bundle without a halo. Many of their objections ascribe to me the view that the members of a trope bundle need to be spatially coincident, which I did not assert in the paper they quote but in fact took some pains to criticise. Hence I am not committed to the non-existence of substantial non-spatial souls, though I am not rushing to sign up to that view.

They further claim that my theory is inconsistent in the following way. (I change their example but keep the point. For present purposes it does not matter whether the example is scientifically wholly accurate.) Consider a single atom of hydrogen well away from other atoms, containing the usual nucleus of a single protons and a single orbital electron. The proton is positively charged, that is, its bundle contains a positive charge trope. The electron is negatively charged, that is, in its bundle is a negative charge trope. The relationship of trope to bundle is that of part to whole, and part-whole is transitive. So the positive charge is part of the hydrogen atom bundle, so the hydrogen atom is positively charged, and the negative charge trope is part of the hydrogen atom bundle, so the hydrogen atom is negatively charged. But it is analytically contradictory for an atom to be (simultaneously) both positively and negatively charged. In any case, both are wrong: the atom is electrically neutral.

One way out of this would be to deny that part-whole is transitive, but that is a counsel of despair. Another way would be to deny that the trope-to-bundle relation is part-whole. I have considered this but I do not see what else it could be. It is true that Hoffman and Rosenkranz take as part of their pre-analytic data that a thing's properties are not parts of it, but this datum is defeasible if theory presses hard enough. The way out seems to me to be this. The atom does indeed contain both a negative charge trope and a positive charge trope, but they are not its immediate parts, rather they are trope parts of its more substantial parts, the electron and proton respectively. Mere presence of a trope of a certain kind in a substance is insufficient to ensure that the substance has the property associated with the trope kind. Only if the trope is an immediate part of the substance is this the case. The positive and negative charge tropes are not immediate parts of the atom, and hence they can cancel out overall in this case. Similarly an object composed of many atoms each of which has a certain (small) mass has a much larger mass, not the small one. How tropes from substantial parts interact to produce a Gestalt quality for the larger whole is not something on which one can pronounce *a priori*; the cases have to be examined empirically.

I conclude that Hoffman and Rosenkrantz's attempt to discredit the flexible trope bundle theory is unsuccessful and that until further notice we can continue to regard the notion of substance *qua* independent entity as analysable. The only case which would obviously refute this position would be if a mereologically and logically atomic independent substance could exist. Not even Leibniz's monads would fulfil the second of these requirements, since a monad has successive states. A simple nature would have to be a metaphysical Lone Ranger, possibly without even a dependent companion, able to be the sole thing in the universe. I am not confident that such a simple nature is an inconsistent notion, but on the other hand I can see no use for it outside certain kinds of theology.

4 Revisionary Metaphysics

In *Individuals* Strawson distinguished between descriptive and revisionary metaphysics as follows:

> Descriptive metaphysics is content to describe the actual structure of our thought about the world, revisionary metaphysics is concerned to produce a better structure.[10]

'Revisionary metaphysics', says Strawson further, 'is at the service of descriptive metaphysics.'[11] In so far as any finally correct metaphysical framework for an account of the world will incorporate all the revisions which it will have been necessary to make in the meantime, there is nothing to dissent from here. But Strawson meant something more, namely that there is a core of metaphysical propositions and concepts which are not subject to revision, and which revisionist metaphysics, with all the 'intensity of their partial vision' (ibid.) can at most modify peripherally. As we know from above, one of the roles which everyday substances play is that of primary objects of reference, indeed that was much of the point of Strawson's book. But Strawson uses epistemological

---

[10] Strawson (1959), p.9.
[11] Ibid.

arguments to arrive at his metaphysical conclusion, and a metaphysician is entitled to claim that this gets the cart before the horse. Everyday substances may perhaps, as Aristotle says, be prior in order of knowledge, but that does not mean they are prior in the order of being. The thrust of early Greek naturalism and of natural science since the seventeenth century has been to attempt to explain what everyday substances are and how they behave in terms of other, more fundamental entities, which are far from first in the order of knowledge. A metaphysical scheme which describes the world by taking these more fundamental things into account cannot count as descriptive, unless and until that scheme become the one embodying 'the actual structure of our thought about the world.' Since natural science when appended to commonsense knowledge provides us with a more comprehensive and more satisfactory picture of the world than commonsense knowledge alone, a metaphysician aiming at a comprehensive and fundamental metaphysical framework is required to take the deliverances of established natural science into account, to the extent that their metaphysics does not contradict entrenched scientific results. The leading edge of metaphysics will therefore be revisionary unless and until we reach the final goal. Nor need revisionary metaphysics, as Strawson suggests, be partial. On the contrary, a metaphysics which does not aspire to universality does not deserve the name, and it is the conceptual scheme inherent in commonsense talk that will be incomplete for lack of coverage of outlying regions inaccessible to common sense.

4.1 Quantum Phenomena

The best theory we have of what makes up everyday substances and explains how they behave as they do is quantum mechanics. In quantum mechanics we lose identifiable individuals in the sense of Aristotle. This was recognised very early: here is what Schrödinger has to say:

> the elementary particle is not an individual; it cannot be identified, it lacks 'sameness'. The fact is known to every physicist … In technical language it is covered by saying the particles 'obey' new-fangled statistics, either Einstein-Bose or Fermi-Dirac statistics. The implication, far from obvious, is that the unsuspected epithet 'this' is not quite properly applicable

to, say, an electron, except with caution, in a restricted sense, and sometimes not at all.[12]

The more we investigate the properties of matter and energy the less quantities of them look like reidentifiable substances. Photons, obeying Bose-Einstein statistics, tend to congregate in the same place at the same time and in the same state: this is the principle behind lasers. Even electrons, which, as fermions, cannot be in exactly the same state as one another, are still, when entangled, such that there is no fact of the matter which is which: they are not nameable distinct individuals. In standard quantum mechanics we can at least say of the electrons orbiting a helium nucleus that there are two of them. In quantum field theory we even lose the countability of particles: states with different numbers of particles are superposed.[13] It used to be thought that quantum phenomena only appear at small scales, but there is no limit to the size of an entangled multi-particle system: a particle pair can be light-years apart when a collapse occurs. Nor is it necessarily a question of low mass or number: at very low temperatures, millions of atoms can be trapped in the same quantum state, forming a so-called Bose-Einstein condensate.[14] The Leibnizian considers as individuals only those things distinguished from all other things by some attribute or other: this means that in most cases individual fundamental particles are not individuals, nor in some circumstances are large aggregates of them. The old substance/attribute model fails to apply at the level of fundamental physical reality. The trope-bundle view fares better here because of its flexibility, but it too may have its limitations.

4.2 Problems in the Mid-World

It might be thought that at least at the mid-world level, the things we perceive around us, the concept of substantial individual, although not scientifically sharp, is at least generally applicable. Unfortunately, finding straightforwardly reidentifiable individual substances turns out to be hard here too. Aristotle's paradigms, the individual organisms, are difficult in two ways. Their kinds or species are determined differently according to the general way in which they reproduce: the standard biological species

---

[12] Schrödinger (1950), pp.109.
[13] Teller (1995), ch. 2.
[14] Irion (1998).

definition only applies to sexually reproducing species at a time or over a short interval, whereas for diachronic purposes, for asexual and parthenogenetic creatures, other ways must be considered of differentiating their fundamental biological kinds.[15] Where it is open how to delimit an object's kind, it can on occasion also be open how to individuate members of that kind. More importantly, the bounds of individual organisms may be uncertain or arbitrary. Many creatures such as sponges, slime moulds, termite colonies, Portuguese men o' war, lichens, tree grafts and more are dubiously individual organisms: they may be connected multiplicities or colonies, or hover on the boundaries between individuals and collectives. It seems somehow artificial to force the question 'one individual or many?' on them: they are organised at different levels in different ways (and falling under different sortal terms) and there may be no distinguished level dictating the boundaries of 'the' biological individual.

Organisms, with their continual energy and matter exchange with the environment, lack perfectly clear boundaries. Even large inorganic things pose difficulties. A large object like the sun has no natural skin or other surface discontinuity, so that there are at any time many connected masses of matter and energy of which it is indeterminate whether they are its parts or not.[16] Geographical features such as mountains, islands, cities and rivers are all to a greater or lesser extent vague.[17] Whereas vagueness of predicates may be considered a necessary and perhaps largely benign product of human inexactness and lack of discrimination, the vagueness attending the part-predicate feeds its way down to the metaphysics, because if it is indeterminate what an object's part are, it can be indeterminate which object it is, if any.

Cartesians may wish to cite the self as one clear-cut case of an unambiguously identifiable individual with a clear identity. Sadly for them, the concept of the identity of the self or person is one of the most fraught: not only do there appear to be natural violations of the natural groupings of experiences by owner which are its standard test,[18] the concept of a person appears at least as much endowed with open texture as any we use.[19]

---

[15] See e.g. the papers in Ereshefsky (ed.) (1992).
[16] For this example and a theory of vague objects generally see Simons (forthcoming).
[17] The problem concerns geographers: see Burrough and Frank (eds.) (1996).
[18] See Wilkes (1988).
[19] See Parfit (1984).

5 Whither Substance?

Fundamental particles, organisms, persons, artifacts, geographical features and heavenly bodies, not to mention socio-political entities like firms and states, and all abstract entities, which have not even been considered here, all raise serious or even insoluble difficulties when considered as metaphysical substances. Suddenly it begins to look as though substance, far from being a widely applicable commonplace, is a concept rarely if ever fulfilled, an idealized limit of little or no use to metaphysics.

This conclusion should I think be accepted. Future metaphysics worthy of the name will need to be revisionary, and the concept *substance* will feature within it, at best, as a derivative construct. It is premature to say how such a future revisionary metaphysics will look, but it will need to both accommodate the advances of science as well as provide the platform for showing how we and our commonsense knowledge, including the knowledge of what have been thought of as individual substances, have a place within the same overall scheme. Substance will not be simply discredited, but its role as a fundamental metaphysical primitive is gone forever. Its formal moments, the notions of independence, of persistence, of unity and integrity, of discernibility, will need to be taken account of, but they will be analytical factors out of which the everyday notion is obtained, probably with some admixture of epistemological content in order to match the notion to its paradigm examples.

Aristotelian and Scholastic metaphysics assumed without argument a fundamental harmony between the world as it is in itself on the one hand and our knowledge of it, concepts for it and language for talking about it on the other. Kant questioned the direction of fit, turning it around so that the world fits our concepts and intuitions rather than vice versa, but he maintained the harmony. Wittgenstein, both early and late, maintained the harmony of language and world, and it is assumed by nearly all linguistically-inspired metaphysics, of whatever variety. As we have seen from only a sample, there are many ways in which language fails to mirror reality. If there is any mirroring at all, it is not between language and world but between language and experience. We are the language-moulders and users, and we learn language through our experience of it and the things it is used about. The world of things in themselves, which is a concept many people, in the grip of the harmony thesis, will not even accept as legitimate, is obviously not unconnected to our experience and the concepts we employ to make sense of this, but the connection is not one of straightforward mirroring, but more of seeing through a glass darkly. Investigating the nature of the world and our relationship to it is not a task for *a priori* metaphysics but of a science revisable in the light of increasing knowledge about the world and ourselves, *a posteriori* but still with a metaphysical framework of maximal generality at any stage. A metaphysics is a theory of being *qua* being: it is a general theory of everything, or it is nothing at all. The concept *substance* served well enough as long as our knowledge was confined to what we could perceive through the unaided senses and infer from those data. It retains a role as a high-level concept in commonsense knowledge and such disciplines as cognitive science and natural language analysis and processing which remain at this level. As a fundamental metaphysical primitive, it belongs, like the horse and cart, to a bygone age. Neither the vehicle nor the concept will take us to the stars.

School of Philosophy
University of Leeds
Leeds LS2 9JT
UK
p.m.simons@leeds.ac.uk

References

Broad, C. D. (1933). *An Examination of McTaggart's Philosophy* vol. I (Cambridge: Cambridge University Press).

Burrough, P. A. and Frank, A. U. (eds.) (1996). *Geographic Objects with Indeterminate Boundaries* (London: Taylor & Francis).

Ereshefsky, M. (ed.) (1992). *The Units of Evolution: Essays on the Nature of Species* (Cambridge: MIT Press).

Hoffman, J. and Rosenkrantz, G. (1994). *Substance among other Categories* (Cambridge: Cambridge University Press).

Irion, R. (1998). 'Altered State', *New Scientist* No. 2138, 13 June 1998, pp.26–30.

Lewis, D. K. (1983). *Collected Papers* vol. I (Oxford: Blackwell).

—— (1986). *On the Plurality of Worlds* (Oxford: Blackwell).

Parfit, D. (1984). *Reasons and Persons* (Oxford: Clarendon Press).

Quine, W. V. (1960). *Word and Object* (Cambridge: MIT Press).

Schrödinger, E. (1950). 'What is an elementary particle?', *Endeavour* 9, pp.109–116.

Simons, P. M. (1987). *Parts: A Study in Ontology* (Oxford: Clarendon Press).

—— (1994). 'Particulars in Particular Clothing: Three Trope Theories of Substance', *Philosophy and Phenomenological Research* 54, pp.553–576.

—— (forthcoming). 'Does the sun exist? The problem of vague objects', forthcoming in the *Proceedings of the 20th World Congress of Philosophy*, Boston, 1998.

Simons, P. M. and Ganthaler, H. (1987). 'Bernard Bolzanos kosmologischer Gottesbeweis', *Philosophia Naturalis* 24, pp.469–475.

Strawson, P. F. (1959). *Individuals: An Essay in Descriptive Metaphysics* (London: Methuen).
Teller, P. (1995). *An Interpretive Introduction to Quantum Field Theory* (Cambridge: MIT Press).
Wilkes, K. V. (1988). *Real people: Personal Identity without Thought Experiments* (Oxford: Clarendon Press).

III

A RETURN TO FORM IN THE PHILOSOPHY OF MIND [1]

John Haldane

Abstract

In recent decades philosophy of mind has undergone a number of important transformations. In the first part of this essay I review a survey of the subject provided by Daniel Dennett some twenty years ago and consider the current state of affairs. Notwithstanding the rise of physicalist causal theories, the field now displays a degree of diversity that suggests disarray. In the second part of the essay I examine three central issues: the nature of persons, of thought, and of action, and present a series of hylomorphic accounts of each.

Part One: Forward to the Present

Twenty years ago, Daniel Dennett took stock of the then current state of the philosophy of mind. Certain aspects of his overview are particularly relevant to my present concerns. He began by noting that the field was one of the most actively worked in contemporary philosophy; that over the period many of the topics had been transformed; and that new concerns had emerged that had no obvious ancestors in earlier enquiry. Later, in the course of discussing versions of physicalist identity theory, he paused briefly to mention dualism, only to dismiss it and move on. In his own words 'it is widely granted these days that dualism is not a serious view to contend with, but rather a cliff over which to push one's opponents'.[2] Dennett's concludes the overview with alternative prognoses: the optimistic one is that the various lines of enquiry will converge upon a broad version of physicalist

---

[1] In addition to the *Ratio* conference held at the University of Reading, versions of this material were presented to audiences at Emory University, Fordham University, at the Centre for the Philosophy of Science, University of Pittsburgh, and at the University of Edinburgh. I am grateful to David Oderberg, Robert McCauley, John Conley, James Lennox, and Stephen Priest for the invitations to speak on these occasions and to members of the audiences for their observations. I am also grateful to John Zeis for written comments on a related talk given at SUNY Buffalo.
[2] See D. Dennett, 'Current Issues in the Philosophy of Mind', *American Philosophical Quarterly* 15 (1978), pp.249–61.

functionalism; the realistic one is that this consensus will be replaced by other doctrines and difficulties.

If anything, the study of the nature of mind has become more dominant within philosophy subsequent to Dennett's essay. It is appropriate, therefore, to consider how things stand two decades later. There has been more continuity than revolution; though for reasons that will emerge I think we may have reached a significant juncture. The period with which Dennett was concerned included the rise of causal and naturalistic views, self-consciously directed against earlier positions that sought to remove mind from the sphere of causal mechanism. Ryle in one manner, Wittgenstein in another, and J. L. Austin in a third had developed ways of understanding psychological discourse that placed it in the sphere of (implicitly social) description and evaluation. Describing someone's beliefs or reasons for action on these accounts is not a matter of postulating – let alone identifying – certain internal states that are related to behaviour as cause to effect. Rather one is characterising that behaviour in ways that show it to be intelligible, reliable, or otherwise part of the life of a rational animal. (This view will re-emerge later.)

It would not be an exaggeration to say that by the early 1960s broadly hermeneutic views – though not described as such – had come to be orthodox among the generation of British and British-trained philosophers working in the wake of Austin, Ryle and Wittgenstein. They even had a 'Truth Society' publication series: *Studies in Philosophical Psychology* (Routledge & Kegan Paul) under the general editorship of R. F. Holland. This included a string of classics: Peter Geach, *Mental Acts* (1957), Anthony Kenny, *Action, Emotion and Will* (1963), Norman Malcolm, *Dreaming* (1958), A. I. Melden, *Free Action* (1961), and Peter Winch, *The Idea of a Social Science* (1958). The reception of these works was generally not less than favourable, and often they were heralded as launching philosophy of psychology as a field of conceptual enquiry.

Even as they were being published, however, the seed of a counter-movement was being sown. In the same year (1963) as saw the appearance of Kenny's *Action, Emotion and Will*, the *Journal of Philosophy* published Donald Davidson's 'Actions, Reasons and Causes'. Davidson is rightly highly regarded as a philosopher of mind, but attention has tended to focus on direct presentations of his anomalous monism such as is given in 'Mental Events'. This appeared seven years after 'Actions,

Reasons and Causes' and makes use of a powerful idea first presented there. The idea in question is simple and brilliant: the fact that a reason renders intelligible the action it is invoked to explain does not preclude the having of the reason being a cause of the behaviour in question. In short, hermeneutics does not exclude causality. Famously Davidson goes on to argue that it actually requires it, since nothing will be an explanation of what happened unless it specifies a cause of it. Otherwise expressed, his point is that the notions of *reason to* and of *reason why* are not the same and that only the latter explains the performance of an action. This is, I think, a stroke of genius which – linked to the point which he took from the hermeneuticists, viz. that rationalisation is not lawlike – then enabled him to derive the very widely discussed thesis that interacting mental and physical events instantiate physical laws and hence are both physical.

Here I am not subscribing to Davidson's views, only paying homage to his deep creativity as a thinker. Evidence of the power of his central ideas is provided by the history of subsequent developments. During the period with which Dennett was concerned, the non-causal hermeneuticists lost considerable ground both internationally because of the rise of interest in philosophy of mind among North American thinkers, who have always been more naturalistically inclined, and in Britain because of the apparent plausibility and fecundity of Davidsonian ideas. Dennett barely gives Davidson a mention – the sole reference being to 'Mental Events', and then only as one of a group of publications by different authors. This is not, I think, out of any lack of generosity but because at the time of writing the Davidsonian view was still being received and it appeared as only one of a number of significant developments.

This brings me to the 'optimistic prognosis' and the current state of philosophy of mind. Reading Dennett's overview, knowing what one does about his own position which has been much elaborated in the intervening years, and recognising the compositional conventions appropriate to surveys, it is tempting to dismiss his 'more realistic prediction', that the physicalist consensus will prove 'as evanescent as its predecessors', as more of a well-mannered gesture than an expression of personal conviction. Most of Dennett's essay is taken up with describing various ways in which logical behaviourism came to be rejected and a naturalistic consensus began to take shape. Subsequent developments have seemed to confirm that consensus, though in this decade evidence of fragmentation has been apparent. I believe that the full significance of this fragmentation has not yet been widely appreciated.

First the consensus. Davidson seemed to have shown that it was not only possible to have the anomality of rational explanation with the nomologicality of causality, but that they went together, and taken jointly entailed physicalism. Putnam and others were credited with recognising – perhaps for the first time – that psychological concepts are functional ones and imply no ontology for their realisers. This could be understood as showing that as it had traditionally been conceived of, the mind-body problem was besides the point so far as understanding psychological predicates and the descriptions and explanations in which they feature was concerned. That indeed was Putnam's view. But it was not long before the argument emerged that functions are causal roles, and that the only way these could be discharged is through physical processes. Indeed, I think there was less often an argument than a subsumption of functionality under physicality. So for all that Putnam had claimed to side-step the old ontological issue, those who adopted functionalism saw it as an endorsement of physicalism. Even those who came to be associated with resistance to identity theory – such as Kripke and Nagel – were taken, at most, to have demonstrated the untenability of type-type identification. In this way they were viewed as more or less part of the consensus that the truth about mental events is that they are physical events, but that those features in virtue of which they are properly classified as mental (function, intentional content, qualitative feel or whatever) are distinct from those by which they are classified as physical.

Expectation of something like this convergence underlies Dennett's optimistic prognosis. As I have said, I think that developments after 1978 proceeded further in this direction. Yet the movement towards naturalism has not carried everyone with it. There have been forces of resistance representing earlier positions, defectors to these views, and an increasing number of unaligned parties who wonder whether the enterprise of understanding the mind and placing it in nature is an intellectually feasible one. Consider in this connection Dennett's remark that 'dualism is not a serious view to contend with'. Encouragement for that verdict may have been provided by the absence of contemporary advocates. Certainly Dennett's bibliography of 114 items includes no avowedly dualist work. A rather different pictures emerges, however, if one looks at the current literature. Admittedly there are few advocates of unqualified substance dualism, but that was never a majority view in the twentieth century, and as historical scholarship has shown even Descartes was less than sure how best to express his own ideas about the mind-body relationship.

If we relax the conditions on being a 'dualist' then quite a number of philosophers now seem to be describable as such. In 1994 Blackwell published an anthology entitled *The Mind-Body Problem: A Guide to the Current Debate.* This contains twenty seven contributions, some reprints and abridgements, and some new essays. The whole is organised in five sections. Sections IV and V are entitled 'Beyond Reductive Naturalism' and 'Subjectivity, Incorrigibility, and Dualism', respectively; between them they contain almost half the essays in the book. In the last section several well-known and respected philosophers argue to one or another dualist position. Some, such as John Foster and Richard Swinburne, have even developed book length presentations of dualism, as have others not represented in the anthology.[3]

This suggests one difference between the years covered by Dennett's survey and the subsequent period: dualism has to be contended with. More significant, however, is the change in general mood which has provided a context in which a revival of dualism seems feasible. Whatever his expressed conclusions, the overall tone of Dennett's writing there and since is one of progress and optimism. More precisely the suggestion is that now that philosophy of mind has been put on a proper footing we can expect to get somewhere. Logical behaviourism and mind-body dualism having been set aside the ground was clear to build upon, and the nature of the emerging edifice is unquestionably 'naturalistic'. The chief building blocks of this structure are *physicalism,* understood as the claim that every substance is a physical substance (either primitively or by linear combination) and *causalism,* the last being the thesis that the mind (however this is

---

[3]   See John Foster, *The Immaterial Self: A Defence of the Cartesian Dualist Conception of the Mind* (London: Routledge, 1991), and Richard Swinburne, *The Evolution of the Soul* (Oxford: Clarendon Press, 1986). See also the essays in H. Robinson (ed.), *Objections to Physicalism* (Oxford: Clarendon Press, 1993); and for book length presentations of non-Cartesian dualism see W. D. Hart, *The Engines of the Soul* (Cambridge: Cambridge University Press, 1988); and E. J. Lowe, *Subjects of Experience* (Cambridge: Cambridge University Press, 1996).

to be understood) is a many-part operating system in which psychological items stand in relations of efficient causation to inputs from the environment, to one another and to behavioural outputs.

This chimes very well with the core of Davidson's position (the anomaly of the mental, while obviously important to him, is something additional). Although his emphasis on the non-reducibility of the psychological to the physical may go some way towards accounting for the fact, it is worth remarking that Davidson has had little to say about physicalism as such; generally he moves from 'physical' to 'physical concepts' and then lists a few such as length, weight and temperature. By contrast he is vocal on behalf of the idea of causation and its importance. In fact he has characterised his essays on actions, events and mind as being unified both in theme and general thesis by this idea:

> The theme is the role of causal concepts in the description and explanation of human action. The thesis is that the ordinary notion of cause which enters into scientific or common-sense accounts of non-psychological affairs is essential also to the understanding of what it is to act for a reason ... Cause is the cement of the universe; the concept of cause is what holds together our picture of the universe, a picture that would otherwise disintegrate into a diptych of the mental and the physical.[4]

It is ironic, therefore, that physical causality should have been invoked in what has become a fairly sustained attack on Davidson's position and on related versions of non-reductive physicalism. Various authors are associated with this criticism including Dretske, Haugeland, Honderich, Kim, and Stoutland. They differ between themselves but they are agreed that Davidson's insistence on the non-reducibility of the mental, combined with the claim that the laws under which mental-physical interaction occurs are physical ones, entails the inefficacy of mental attributes. Put another way, while Davidson's position allows that those events which are mental are causally related to inputs and outputs, the relations in question hold not in virtue of their mentality but on account of their physicality. The resulting

---

[4] See Donald Davidson, *Essays on Actions & Events* (Oxford: Clarendon Press, 1980) p. xi.

options seem to be to accept epiphenomenalism, which contradicts the starting point of the theory, viz. that there is mental-physical interaction, or else to endorse the reduction of the mental to the physical, which contradicts the anomality thesis.

Davidson has responded forcefully to arguments of this sort but I have to say that I find his responses implausible.[5] So too, it would appear, do others. Standing back from the detailed dialectic it seems clear why the very enterprise was so appealing but also why it seemed doomed from the outset. Philosophy of mind from the early 1970s onwards moved towards the consensus I described earlier: that of non-reductive physicalism or token-identity theory. It did so because dualism seemed evidently false; yet type identity faced counterexamples from, for example, the multiple physical-realisability of mental states, and efforts to secure reduction via disjunctive type-identification seem at best hopelessly ad hoc and not to yield genuinely projectible pairings. What was wanted was the following: 1) *a duality of attributes*; 2) *a monism of bearers*; 3) *some sort of determination relation between the physicality of a bearer and the mentality of an attribute*; yet 4) *non-reducibility of the latter to the former*. In short, the benefits of dualism without its costs, or the virtues of physicalism without its liabilities.

If one thinks with Davidson's critics that these are impossible combinations the question becomes that of where to move next, and what is interesting is that different authors have gone in quite different directions. Kim upholds the merits of a reductive identity theory;[6] Haugeland[7] and Stoutland[8] appear to favour a return to non-realist versions of hermeneuticism; John McDowell, who takes the anomaly of the mental from Davidson but rejects his commitment to the 'prejudice of' (*sic*) the nomologicality of causation, advances a version of event

---

[5] See, for example, 'Problems in the Explanation of Action' in P. Pettit, R. Sylvan and J. Norman (eds.), *Metaphysics and Morality* (Oxford: Blackwell, 1987), pp.35–49; and 'Thinking Causes' in John Heil and Alfred Mele (eds.), *Mental Causation* (Oxford: Clarendon Press, 1993), pp.3–17.

[6] See Jaegwon Kim, *Supervenience and Mind* (Cambridge: Cambridge University Press, 1993).

[7] See the introduction and essays in John Haugeland, *Having Thought* (Cambridge, MA: Harvard University Press, 1998).

[8] See Frederick Stoutland, 'Davidson on Intentional Behaviour', in Ernest LePore and Brian McLaughlin (eds.), *Actions and Events* (Oxford: Blackwell, 1985), pp.44–59; and 'On Not Being a Behaviourist', in Lars Hertzberg and Juhani Pietarinen (eds.), *Perspectives on Human Conduct* (Leiden: E. J. Brill, 1988), pp.37–60.

dualism;[9] and Paul Churchland continues to deny that there are any psychological features to be accounted for.[10] This contrasting selection hardly exhausts the range of views currently to be found among professional philosophers. I mentioned that dualism is back on the scene and my estimate is that every one of the positions indicated in the following two-part diagram now has defenders. (I leave it as an interesting exercise for the reader to assign individual philosophers to these positions.) One might regard this as a healthy sign of pluralism, but given the fundamental character of what is at issue I believe it is more accurately taken as showing that as a group we contemporary philosophers of mind really do not know what to think. There is wisdom in Kripke's observation voiced almost thirty years ago: ' I regard the mind-body problem as wide open and extremely confusing'.[11]

Basic Options in the Philosophy of Mind

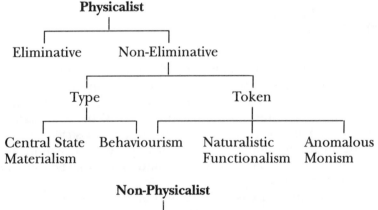

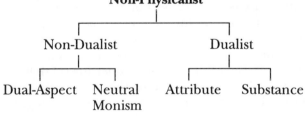

[9] See John McDowell, 'Functionalism and Anomalous Monism', in LePore and McLaughlin (eds.), *Actions and Events*, pp.387–98; reprinted in J. McDowell, *Mind, Value and Reality* (Harvard: Harvard University Press, 1998).

[10] See Paul Churchland and Patricia Churchland, *On the Contrary: Critical Essays 1987–1997* (Cambridge, MA: MIT Press, 1998).

[11] See Saul Kripke, *Naming and Necessity* (Oxford: Blackwell, 1980), p. 155, note 77.

To these one might add *Quietism*, which is the view, often associated with followers of Wittgenstein, that there is nothing (philosophical) to be said; and *Scepticism*, the opinion advanced by Colin McGinn, following certain suggestions of Chomsky and Nagel, that such are our natural cognitive limitations that there is nothing *we* can say.[12]

Part Two: Back to the Future

Occupancy of one or other of the positions roughly identified in the diagram has traditionally been philosophically motivated by the attempt to solve the mind-body problem. This, of course, is not the only metaphysical issue in the philosophy of mind. In fact, I suggest it is useful to see the field as composed of three overlapping areas each defined by the need to account for the nature of something broadly psychological. These three problems are as follows:

1) *The Nature of Persons;*
2) *The Nature of Thought;*
3) *The Nature of Action.*

The first is the traditional locus of the mind-body problem, but when one considers sense-cognition it soon becomes evident that there is a difficulty about the connection between perception and sensation: are they distinct? identical? or is there a relationship of some other sort? and is thought a physical process? Likewise in asking about the relationship between action and movement very similar issues arise and one quickly faces an 'agent-body problem'.

Each of the three areas is the subject of extensive discussion in contemporary philosophy. Some authors make connections between them but many do not. In this part of the essay I will proceed boldly and suggest that progress on each may be achieved by making use of the ancient doctrine of hylomorphism. Though I shall not pursue the further issue now, I think that the proper deployment of that idea suggests the integration of the three areas mentioned through the metaphysical priority of the first. Put another way, a correct account of the nature of persons will include, as essential aspects, accounts of the nature

---

[12] For an up-to-date and balanced survey of the field see John Heil, *Philosophy of Mind: A Contemporary Introduction* (London: Routledge, 1998).

of thought and of action, since these are the primary modes of activity of those beings whose nature is that of persons. As the medieval scholastics, following Aristotle, were wont to say, 'acting follows upon being' and 'things are specified by their powers'.[13]

Before proceeding, let me say how I understand the notions of form and matter and the motivation for their introduction. My view is broadly Aristotelian though it invokes elements from Aquinas which are at least not explicit in Aristotle, and arguably may not be there at all. In allowing for their absence, however, I am not suggesting the possibility that they are incompatible with Aristotle's conception. In fact the ideas in question are ones that pre-date Aristotle and are, I believe, what one arrives at if one thinks about the possibility of there being any things, or any thoughts of things.

The Pre-Socratics asked very broad metaphysical questions and delivered equally wide-ranging answers. One such question is 'what is the nature of reality?'. Anaximander speculated that the original state of things was that of an undifferentiated mass; a vast extent of unstructured some-such. This he termed the 'indefinite' or the 'undifferentiated' (the *apeiron)*. The question then became that of the source of the structure apparent in the world. Subsequently Pythagoras, who adopted the notion of the *apeiron,* thought of emergent structure in mathematical terms. Thus he came to the view that the making of the *kosmos* involved the imposition of limit (*peras*) upon the undifferentiated, so as to produced the structured (*peperasmenon).* The Pre-Socratics thought in terms of a genesis, but the general principle can be abstracted from any historical process of production. Moreover, no sense can be made of a something about which nothing can be said; a pure *apeiron* would resist any kind of subject/predicate description. This I take to show that a condition of there being something for thought to take hold of is that the something has structure. Equivalently, a condition of there being thought is that there be relevant structuring principles (sortal and characterising concepts plus logical constants).

So we arrive at hylomorphic analysis. Every particular may be understood in terms of the instantiation of a formal principle. Its

[13] See for example Aristotle, *De Anima*, Book II, Ch. IV, and Aquinas's commentary. Both texts appear in Kenelm Foster and Silvester Humphries (trs.), *Aristotle's De Anima in the Version of William of Moerbeke and the Commentary of St Thomas Aquinas* (London: Routledge and Kegan Paul, 1951).

form makes it to be the kind of thing it is, providing its definitive structure, its characteristic powers and liabilities, and so on. However, since, ex hypothesi, things of the same specific sort have formally identical principles there arises the question of numerical difference. The analysis is completed by introducing the idea of matter as that which is structured and is the basis of numerical individuation within species. Their forms make two men alike (*qua* men); their matter makes them distinct (*qua* individual men). Speaking, as I just have, of the 'matter' of living things it is tempting to proceed by iterative analysis so as to be led, via the form and matter of flesh and bones, and then of tissue fibre and chemical compounds, etc., to the infamous idea of *prime matter* – stuff of no kind.

This is avoidable. Think again of the Pythagorean principle: structure conjoined with absence of structure constitutes something structured. Considered in the abstract it becomes clear that the unstructured, while not a something, is not a mere nothing. It is the possibility or potentiality for the reception of structure, and that structure stands to it as an actualising principle. This, I suggest (employing Aquinas's potency/act distinction)[14] is how at the metaphysical level we should think of matter and form. The first is a potentiality for the reception of the second, the second a determinate actualisation of this potentiality. Next, if we consider various kinds of forms we can ask about the kinds of possibility there are for their actualisation or instantiation. In the case of concrete particulars the answer would appear to be 'spatio-temporality', or whatever at the most fundamental level constitutes the empirical domain. But, of course, empirical reality always comes informed by some structure (and that necessarily, for recall the earlier remarks about the *apeiron*). So we need to distinguish between a) matter as the condition of the possibility of the actuality of form (*materia prima*); and b) matter as a particular empirical medium (*materia signata*). Matter in the first sense is not an empirical concept; matter in the second sense is the most general empirical concept.

One odd-sounding, but in fact coherent, implication of this is

---

[14] See, for example, Aquinas, 'On the Principles of Nature', in Timothy McDermott, *Thomas Aquinas: Selected Philosophical Writings* (Oxford: Oxford University Press, 1993): 'Now just as anything potential can be called *material*, so anything that gives existence ... can be called *form*', p. 68.

that it is an open question whether there is any immaterial matter. The initial impression of contradiction is removed when we see that this is now reformulable as asking whether there may be non-empirical potentialities for the reception of form. I will come to what I believe to be one such possibility very shortly, but let me note that the analysis I have offered allows for a charitable interpretation of a view held in the Middle Ages. Peter Geach writes

> Some Scholastics held that just as two pennies or two cats differ by being different bits of matter, so human souls differ by containing different 'spiritual matter'. Aquinas regarded this idea as self-contradictory; it is at any rate much too obscure to count as establishing a possibility of distinct disembodied souls.[15]

Though he does not say so, I imagine Geach has in mind Aquinas's disagreement with Bonaventure. In his *Commentary on the Sentences* (of Peter Lombard), Bonaventure writes that 'the rational soul is the principle and form of the human body' and then adds (following in a tradition begun a century earlier by Avicebron (Ibn Gebirol)) that the soul itself is hylomorphically composed of spiritual form and spiritual matter (*Super libros sententiarum*, 18). In the *Summa*, Aquinas asks 'whether the soul is composed of form and matter' and argues that it is not (*Summa Theologiae*, Ia, q. 75, a 5). His reasons are cogent so far as the possibility of a plurality of individual souls is concerned, but someone who was willing to countenance the old idea of a single universal soul might hold on to the idea that this is realised in 'spiritual matter'. Needless to say, I am not endorsing that proposal, but I do wish to prepare the ground for the suggestion that there are non-empirical modes of receiving forms.

The nature of persons and of thought as these might be viewed from the perspective of a broadly Aristotelian hylomorphism are matters I have discussed in other places. Here I shall develop these suggestions somewhat briefly, so as to relate them to the general scheme of possibilities represented above, and then turn to consider the particular issue of causation and action. Readers requiring more in the way of supporting argumentation may care

[15] See Peter Geach, 'Immortality', in his *God and the Soul* (London: Routledge & Kegan Paul, 1969), pp.17–29, at p. 23.

to consult my earlier discussions – though I have no illusion that they will be satisfied by them.[16]

The problem of the nature of thought has several aspects of which two are prominent. What is the implication of the correct account of intentionality for the traditional issue of realism vs. representationalism? and what is the character and source of the components and the structure of thought (concepts and rationality, respectively)? It is characteristic of contemporary accounts of intentionality – be they internalist or externalist – that they view the originating relationship between object and thought in terms of the efficacy of the former in producing the latter. Crudely, we are to understand thoughts as prompted by the objects they are about, as those objects or their effects impinge upon our senses, or as facts about them are relayed by chains of communication going back to such impingements.

As one reflects upon this view it is hard not to feel the prospects of realism in cognition slipping away. In contemporary debates about intentionality it is possible to distinguish two positions which I shall label 'old' and 'new' versions of 'representationalism'. According to the first, the immediate objects of thought are images, ideas or sentences. These are themselves foci of cognition, and external reference is mediated by them (via a relationship of picturing (natural resemblance) or symbolism (whatever that might be and however it might be accounted for)). On standard interpretations Descartes and Locke are old-style representationalists, as, in some of their pronouncements, are Hartry Field and Jerry Fodor.[17] According to the second position, while mental representations mediate between the thinker and reality they are not themselves objects of cognition. So, while it may that in order to think about some state of affairs it has to be the case that there is some proposition-like representation in

---

[16] See John Haldane, 'Folk Psychology and the Explanation of Human Behaviour', *Proceedings of the Aristotelian Society*, Supplementary Volume 62 (1988), pp.223–54; 'Mind-World Identity Theory and the Anti-Realist Challenge' in John Haldane and Crispin Wright (eds.), *Reality, Representation and Projection* (New York: Oxford University Press, 1993), pp.15–37; 'The Life of Signs', *Review of Metaphysics* 47 (1994), pp.451–70; 'Intentionality and One-Sided Relations', *Ratio* 11 (1996), pp.95–114; 'Rational and Other Animals', in A. O'Hear (ed.), *Verstehen and Humane Understanding* (Cambridge: Cambridge University Press, 1996), pp.17–28; and 'Forms of Thought', in Lewis Hahn (ed.), *The Philosophy of Roderick Chisholm* (Chicago: Open Court, 1997), pp.149–70.

[17] See, for example, J. Fodor, *Representations: Philosophical Essays on the Foundations of Cognitive Science* (Brighton: Harvester, 1981); and 'Mental Representation: An Introduction', in N. Rescher (ed.), *Scientific Inquiry in Philosophical Perspective* (New York: University Press of America, 1987), pp.105–28.

the thinker's mind it does not follow that the thinker cognises the state of affairs by entertaining a representation. Rather the tokening of a propositional content by a mental sentence constitutes the thought, and reference is secured via the relationship between this and the external reality.[18]

Whatever the relative merits of these positions both have the consequence that mind is somewhat removed from the world. For even if a complete representationalist account of thought must make a connection between a subject's internal states and the external world (and not every theory of this sort accepts that requirement) the connection can only be *extrinsic*, a matter of efficient causation. In his Dewey Lectures Hilary Putnam draws upon terminology adopted from John McDowell in order to make a similar critical point. He writes:

> McDowell argues persuasively that this picture [old representationalism], whether in its classical version or in its modern materialist version, is disastrous for just about every part of metaphysics and epistemology. In McDowell's terminology the key assumption responsible for the disaster is the idea that there has to be an interface [a causal not cognitive linkage] between our cognitive powers and the external world ... Accounts of perception that reject this claim are conventionally referred to as "direct realist" accounts ... But there is less to some versions of "direct realism" than meets the eye. ... All one has to do to be a direct realist (in this sense) about visual experience, for example, is to say, "We don't perceive visual experiences, we have them". ... "We perceive external things – that is, we are caused to have certain subjective experiences in the appropriate way by those external things", such a philosopher can say.[19]

What Putnam refers to here as 'some versions of "direct realism"' is what I have termed 'new versions of representationalism'. One might ask, however, what the alternative may be. Again following McDowell, but also under the influence of William

---

[18] Such a view is canvassed by Robert Stecker in criticism of my interpretation and endorsement of Thomas Reid's opposition to the doctrine of ideas. See Robert Stecker, 'Does Reid Reject/Refute the Representational theory of Mind?', *Pacific Philosophical Quarterly* 73 (1992), pp.174–84. I reply in 'Whose Theory? Which Representations?', *Pacific Philosophical Quarterly* 74 (1993), pp.247–57.

[19] See Hilary Putnam, 'Sense, Nonsense, and the Senses: An Inquiry into the Powers of the Human Mind', *Journal of Philosophy* 91(1994), pp.445–517, at pp.453–4.

James, Putnam advances what he calls *natural realism*: the view that 'successful perception is just a seeing, or hearing, or feeling, etc., of things "out there" and not a mere affectation of a person's subjectivity by those things'.[20]

I agree with this but what I find missing from Putnam's discussion (and indeed from McDowell's treatment of intentionality)[21] is any explicit account of how this is possible. Elsewhere I have urged the merit of the maxim 'no epistemology without ontology'[22] and in this context the requirement is to say what else grounds the cognition of reality if not the effects of objects upon our senses, 'the affectation of our subjectivity'. Clearly input from the world is relevant and is in part at least a matter of efficient causation. However, if there is to be the sort of conformity of mind to thing which Putnam and McDowell seek, then I can only see this being provided according to an account of the sort developed by Aquinas when he writes that the intellect in act is the intelligible in act; or less scholastically, that a thought will only be of a thing when it is formally identical with it; when what we think and what is thought are the same.[23]

What does this mean? And how is it possible? It means that when I think of something, that which makes my thought to be the kind of thought it is – a dog-thought, say – is formally identical to that which makes the object of my thought to be the kind of thing it is, a dog. Each actuality (thought and object) has a structuring principle (concept and substantial form); and these principles, though distinct in the modes of their actualisation, are specifically alike. The form of dog exists naturally and substantially (*in esse naturale*) in the dog, and intentionally and predicatively (*in esse intentionale*) in the thought. To make full sense of this we need to extend standard Aristotelian ontology to include three different kinds of existents (1 – 3) and three kinds

---

[20] Putnam, 'Sense, Nonsense and the Senses', p. 454. Later in the lectures Putnam generously notes my own use of the distinction between representations as mental acts, and as cognitive or causal intermediaries: see p. 505; also Haldane, 'Putnam on Intentionality', *Philosophy and Phenomenological Research* 52 (1992), pp.671–82. I hope he might consider the suggestion that formal causation has to be part of a true account of cognition.

[21] See John McDowell, *Mind and World* (Cambridge, MA: Harvard University Press, 1994), Lectures I and II.

[22] See Haldane, 'Rational and Other Animals'.

[23] Compare this with McDowell's Wittgensteinian version of cognitive identity: 'there is no ontological gap between the sort of thing one can ... think, and the sort of thing that can be the case', *Mind and World*, p. 27.

of relation, two being modes of exemplification (4 & 5), the other being one of instantiation (6):

1) *F-ness* – the universal, or form;
2) *The f-ness of X* – a singular case, or instance;
3) *X* – a particular subject;
4) X *exemplifies* F-ness naturally, or is a natural *exemplification* of F-ness;
5) X *exemplifies* F-ness intentionally, or is an intentional *exemplification* of F-ness;
6) The f-ness of X is a natural *case* or *instance* of F-ness.

Contrary to some (mis)representations of the doctrine of intentional existence, when I think of a dog an individual animal does not come to exist in my thought; rather, my thinking takes on a general feature, dogness, which serves as a concept directing me to a particular or to the class. Accordingly, although successive thoughts of the same conceptual type involve numerically distinct exemplifications of the relevant form, these thoughts are not distinct instantiations of that form. For what it is to be an instantiation of F is to be a particularisation of it – a case of F-ness, or the f-ness of a particular, the dogness-of-Lassie, say.

A merit of this view is that it explains what is otherwise a mystery, namely how a thought can be intrinsically related to its object: they share the same form. It also serves, I believe, to save realism from the threat of conceptual relativism. In recent years Putnam has insisted upon an unmediated connection between mind and world. Yet without further specification and explanation this leaves scope for a different kind of scepticism to that traditionally associated with representationalism.

Putnam himself has maintained in a series of well-known publications that permutation arguments leave realism floundering so long as reference is thought of as something fixed objectively.[24] My own diagnosis of the deeper reasoning beneath these essays is that Putnam has presumed that reference-fixing from the side of the world could only be through lines of efficient causation from object to thinker. The problem for the realist, then, is not that

[24] See, for example, Hilary Putnam, 'Models and Reality', in his *Realism and Reason* (Cambridge: Cambridge University Press, 1983), pp.1–25, and 'Model Theory and the "Factuality" of Semantics', in his *Words and Life* (Cambridge, MA: Harvard University Press, 1994), pp.351–75.

there are insufficient such relations, but that there are far too many of them with none standing out as the ground of a reciprocal semantic relation between thinker to object of thought. Consider the vast number of causal lines extending from the world to me when I stand facing a dog and try to say which could constitute a privileged class sufficient to ground reference.

The difficulty is insurmountable so long as one is confined to efficient causation. But a further possibility is now before us. Form exemplified naturally makes the dog to be a dog. Form exemplified intentionally makes my thought of a dog to be a dog-type thought. To this we can add that the intentional exemplification has as a condition of its occurrence some prior natural exemplification. My thought is caused to have its content by the form of the dog.[25] There are, then, three cases of formal causation: *within the natural order, within the intentional order,* and *between the natural and the intentional orders*. It is very important at this point to make clear that formal causation is not a kind of efficient causation, or a rival to it. In late scholastic discussions one sometimes finds authors writing as if forms passed through the air in the manner of effluvia shed from the surfaces of objects. This invites empirical refutation and intellectual parody. But the proposal currently on offer does not require anything like this. We can say instead that the only effecting that goes on, as this is standardly conceived of, is that already known about, *but* that the effecting originates and terminates in formal structures. Efficient causation is the vehicle for the communication of form; form is what structures the object, the thought, and the movement between them. Efficient causation by itself failed to fix reference since what the idea of it omitted was the possibility that it carries form, or, as the scholastics would more accurately say, that it itself is 'subject to formality'. What makes it possible that there be dog-type thoughts is that there be dogs and that the form(s) of the latter has been communicated to the mind of a thinker via formal and efficient causation.

Rather than pursue this issue further I wish to take up, in brief,

---

[25] Putnam worries about the invocation of substantial forms, using the example of dogs to make difficulty for it and to advance his own version of ontological relativity: see 'Aristotle after Wittgenstein', *Words and Life*, pp.62–81. I respond to this in 'On Coming Home to (Metaphysical) Realism', *Philosophy* 71 (1996), pp.287–96.

the question of the general nature of persons, and then to proceed via consideration of the nature of action to address the currently vexed problem of hierarchical causation. Unsurprisingly, a hylomorphist of my persuasion looking at the diagram presented above will be inclined to locate himself under *Non-Dualist, Non-Physicalist*; whether the precise location is *Dual Aspect* or *Neutral Monism* calls for further discussion beyond the scope of this essay, but I favour the former. Why not – setting aside independently motivated prejudice – some version of physicalism? Part of the answer is implicit in what has been said already. Contemporary philosophers of mind confirm the persistence of Cartesianism in their pre-occupation with the status of qualia. I remain agnostic about the possibility of a naturalistic account of qualia and still see merit in an old suggestion of Putnam's that the 'qualitative character' of a sensation, say, is just the physical realisation of a state that has the function of signalling the presence of some feature in the body or in the surrounding environment.[26]

It must seem odd, however, to allow the possibility of token identity for qualia and yet to resist physicalism as a general account of the nature of mind. After all, phenomenal consciousness is widely supposed to be *the* problem for physicalism. I think a degree of romantic subjectivism may lie behind this, as if the key to reality is how we feel in our experiences. At any rate, my principled objection to physicalism pre-dates Descartes and is the Aristotelian-Thomistic one. Wherever there is individuation within kinds there is matter, wherever there is universality matter is absent. In sensation the sense is (efficiently) caused to change and is formally reordered. But in 'taking on' the form of the original object it still does so under material conditions (those of the organ of sense) and so one has particularised qualities: this sensation of redness deriving from that patch of objective redness in the environment. In thought, however, general concepts or universal forms are in operation and given the hylomorphic analysis advanced above this implies that at the intellectual level of information form must be exemplified without empirical instantiation. Abstract thought is structured by

[26] See Hilary Putnam, *Reason, Truth and History* (Cambridge: Cambridge University Press, 1981), ch. 4. Even Nagel should be willing to countenance this suggestion, for a) it is not a functionalist reduction, and b) it is not a conceptual identification. See Thomas Nagel, 'Conceiving the Impossible and the Mind-Body Problem', *Philosophy* 73 (1998), pp.337–52, at pp. 337–8.

universals and universals only exist as such apart from (empirical) matter.[27]

Now recall the principle that acting follows upon being (*agere sequitur esse*). This captures the fact that activities are exercises of powers and that powers belong to substances as parts of their natures. If thought is a non-physical activity as I have argued (admittedly schematically) that it is, then the intellectual powers are not physical; nor, therefore, can be the substance to whose nature the powers belong. Current attribute dualists tend to identify the brain and the higher reaches of the central stem as the physical substance that also has some non-physical properties. But I am urging that a proper understanding of substantiality should lead one to reject the idea that a wholly physical particular could be the bearer of intrinsic attributes that are non-physical. The error of the Cartesian is to suppose that non-physical attributes imply an exclusively incorporeal substance as bearer. In these opposing views we can see the assumption that the only available candidates are material ('physical') substances or immaterial ('psychical') ones. Hylomorphism suggests a way of rejecting that assumption, for it allows the possibility of psycho-physical substances, substances out of whose single nature physical and mental activity flow.

Space does not permit further elaboration of this, but I need to link it with two important issues in the philosophy of action. First, it follows from my account that there can be no general 'other minds' problem, at least if there is no 'other bodies' one. If I can see you walk then I know you are an animal, and if I can hear you talk then I know you are a rational one. If I hear you laugh and see you smile I know you are amused. Acting follows upon being; and if these actions are those of a single substance then what that thing is, is a person. A decade ago, Paul Churchland and I set out opposing views about the nature of psychological explanation. The exchange continued in print for a further round and he recently republished his reply in a collection of critical essays. The reappearance of that exchange is apt to the matter of concern to me here, for there were two main points of disagreement between us. The first is whether action

---

[27] For those preferring a less directly hylomorphic argument, elsewhere I reason from the fact that thoughts involve conceptual modes of presentation to the conclusion that they are not physical: see John Haldane, 'Naturalism and the Problem of Intentionality', *Inquiry* 32 (1989), pp.305–22.

explanation is theoretical as opposed to observational (or perhaps simulatory). The second is whether it is a form of causal explanation, which in the case of 'folk psychology' amounts to the idea that reasons are causes of action. My responses were that it is standardly observational and standardly non-causal – *as causal is standardly understood.*

In cognition the person as subject receives forms, in action the person as agent expresses them. In both cases efficient causation is operating. Light hits the retina, it contracts, electrical impulses are set up in the afferrent nerves, things happen in the brain. Things happen in the brain, impulses pass along efferent nerves, muscles contract, a hand moves. These matters are not in general dispute. The question is, what is their relation to sight and action? I have argued above that if we are to make sense of perception, then we have to bring in formal causation and say that in the chain of efficient cause and effect the formal structure of the object is communicated to the sense, and in thought to the intellect. Perception is hylomorphically constituted, with 'sensibles' standing as forms to the matter of the sense organs.

Likewise action is hylomorphically constituted with intentions standing as forms to the matter of physiological movements. Efficient causation plays its part, but its part in these contexts is conditioned by the forms that govern it. This is why *action* explanation is not 'causal' in the sense universally meant by analytical philosophers of mind and action. When I say that A stood up because he wanted to leave, I am not identifying (by hypothesis) something antecedent to a human movement which was the efficient cause of it. Rather I am identifying it formally (by observation of the agent in the circumstance) and saying that what he was doing was making to leave.

One way of interpreting what I have proposed is as claiming that intentionality plays a role in the production of action additional to physical efficient causation. This formulation should be welcome to critics schooled in the current debates about mental causation, since it will seem to invite the well-rehearsed charge of causal overdetermination and raise the prospect of a retreat to epiphenomenalism of the sort of which Davidson stands accused. In the dock with him are other supervenience theorists and emergence revivalists. Let me recall the prosecution case by means of another diagram.

Suppose we identify a sequence of events and are looking to attach two sets of properties to them, one mental (M) the other physical (P). Suppose further that we say that the mental properties supervene upon the physical ones or are emergent out of them (differences between supervenience and emergence are ultimately not relevant to the charge that is being pressed). Suppose next that we wish to allow that the physical properties in the sequence are causally related (P causes P* etc.). Suppose, finally, we want to say that the mental or more broadly the intentional properties of the events in sequence are also causally related. Then we can represent this in a style familiar from writings by Kim and others:

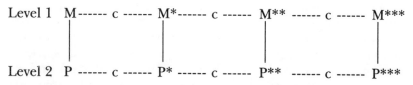

Level 1 M ------ c ------ M* ------ c ------ M** ------ c ------ M***

Level 2 P ------ c ------ P* ------ c ------ P** ------ c ------ P***

Since, by hypothesis, P is naturally or metaphysically sufficient for M and P* is likewise sufficient M*, and moreover P causes P*, it looks as if the attempt to find a role for M in relation to M* faces the dilemma of overdetermination or epiphenomenalism. How can M make a contribution as the advocate of supervenient causation might wish, since the occurrence of M* is already provided for from below? Emergentism envisages downward causation so one might try the suggestion that M brings about M* not directly but by causing P*. That, however, involves denying the causal sufficiency of P for P* and violates the 'causal closure of the physical' (*ccp*).

Much ink has already been spilled on this topic and a number of imaginative suggestions have been canvassed. In a series of characteristically clear and independently minded papers Jonathan Lowe, who appears elsewhere in this volume, has explored the possibility of rejecting the argument (based upon the *ccp*) that if M* has a cause it must be a wholly physical one.[28] There are certainly moves one can make here starting with the observation that the closure principle is question-begging and is not entailed by the conservation laws.

A related line of thought on the problem of emergence and downward causation has been described in a very useful and

---

[28] See E. J. Lowe, 'The Problem of Psychophysical Causation', *Australasian Journal of Philosophy* 70 (1992), pp.263–76, and 'The Causal Autonomy of the Mental', *Mind* 102 (1993), pp.629–44.

widely cited survey essay by Brian McLaughlin on emergentism in earlier British philosophy of mind and science.[29] Consideration of this will lead me to my conclusion. McLaughlin is concerned with the efforts of theorists in the earlier part of the century to combine a number of possibilities. First, everything is made of matter (for convenience let this be particulate). Second, there is no change without change in the basic particles. Third, however, there is a plurality of levels of organisational complexity and of causal powers proper to each level. Following on from the last, the organisational structures endow substances with causal powers additional to those of their particles. In particular, movements of multi-level substances are not due exclusively to motions of their microphysical particles. Structure-relative forces come into play as complexity emerges.

It hardly seems incoherent to suppose that there may be forces other than particle ones. The problem comes with the thought that these might begin to operate in addition to existing forces, for that may appear to be in violation of scientific laws. Movement conforms to the laws of motion, so if the emergent forces make a distinctive contribution to the dynamics of the substances in which they inhere then dynamics will not be reducible to physics (assuming the latter to be confined to the properties of particles). Of itself that might be tolerable, but there is the issue of the conservation of mass and energy. As McLaughlin points out, however, the existence of structural forces can be rendered compatible with conservation principles, so long as it is not supposed that higher level structures have extra mass and so long as it is not assumed that additional energy is created (or destroyed). How, then, can they be effective, i.e. *forces*, at all? An answer lies in the possibility that the physical particles have potential energy that is only released as organisational structures emerge. McLaughlin allows the coherence of this earlier emergentist combination, and its compatibility with basic scientific principles, but is not disposed to believe that what it envisages is true. For he takes it that the empirical evidence shows that in accounting for chemical bonding and micro-biology it is not necessary to appeal to forces other than particle ones.

Further detail or speculation about this possibility is unnecessary in the present context. Instead I wish to suggest how one

---

[29] See B. McLaughlin, 'The Rise and Fall of British Emergentism', in A. Beckermann, H. Flohr, and J. Kim (eds.), *Emergence or Reduction* (Berlin: De Gruyter, 1992), pp.49–93.

might think about form, substance and causality in a way related to but importantly different from what has just been described. As with the emergentists I maintain that structure makes a difference and that there are hierarchies of organisational complexity. In the case of a single unified substance (rather than an aggregate, say) these levels are successively subsumed. In hylomorphic terms there is in such a case only one actual substantial form, though there may be several virtual ones corresponding to lower-level unifications. Activities which in lower-level systems would be attributable to the presence of different kinds of structuring principles are taken under the governance of the higher form. Where I take leave of the earlier emergentism is in rejecting the idea that structure adds or releases force. When discussing cognition I maintained that my thought of a dog is given canine content by being caused to be such by the form of the dog. But I then stressed the importance of not thinking of formal determination as a type of efficient causation. Likewise, I wish to maintain that form may be a determinant of the substantial nature, including the characteristic activities, of a substance without that being a matter of efficiently constraining the location and behaviour of basic particles. Intentionality plays an additional role but not by being an additional force (energy).

Some years ago Elizabeth Anscombe pointed out that the idea of (efficient) causation is not as such that of something deterministic or necessitating.[30] What it means to say that 'c caused e' is that c made e happen. It does not follow from this that were there another situation alike in all relevant antecedent respects the same would happen again. Anscombe's point is an important one but it can be carried further. She, I think, was still inclined to take it for granted that causation was at least patterned if not invariable. So it is, but the possibility of that patterning is not something that can be got out of the idea of efficient causation as such, any more than could be got out the idea of invariability. There is nothing in the idea of physical particles standing in relations of cause and effect that implies, or provides a basis for, the idea of higher level structures behaving in ways characteristic of their natures. Indeed, unless it is taken to be implied by the term 'particles' that what is postulated at the basic level has structure, then order there seems unaccounted for either.

[30] See G. E. M. Anscombe, 'Causality and Determination' in her *Metaphysics and the Philosophy of Mind* (Oxford: Blackwell, 1981), pp.133–47.

I am not denying that there is organisation at that level or that causal relations operating there do so in systematic ways, but I am urging that the possibility of this depends upon the existence of forms or structuring principles. Efficient causation neither implies determination nor excludes randomness, and without formal structure the latter is all that its contingencies could amount to. Once again, what form brings is order, but it does not to do so by pushing things this way or that. Its existence is testified to not by force detectors but by the fact that what exists, and how existents act, exhibit natural order. Without formal causation there would be no regularity, let alone any invariability, in the flow of events, for efficacy alone (or, equivalently, energy as *apeiron*) does not provide it. What forms there are is evident in the structures and patterns of behaviour around us. That is the explanation of the old claim that the subject of science is substantial form.

In the present context the most important example of substantial form is that responsible for the nature and activity of human persons in whom a multitude of functions are brought under the unifying order of thought and action. The role of reason in agency is not as an efficient cause operating to produce movement by way of levels 1 or 2 in the M and P diagram. Rather, it makes a movement to be an action by bestowing upon it an intentional form. And if we ask what made the action happen, then so long as we are indeed dealing with an *action*, the answer is nothing other than the agent's power of actualising the potential of his or her body by subsuming matter-energy already at work under the governance of living form and changing its (formal) character. Resistance to this possibility most likely will arise from the thought that the movement of an agent must already be determined (or probabilified) antecedently and from below – by the facts of physical causation – but I cannot see that this is anything other than a physicalist prejudice and it is certainly question-begging. From the fact that physics is applicable to human movement it does not follow that action is reducible to it, or to it plus efficient mental causation.

Dennett wrote of new concerns having emerged in the philosophy of mind that had no obvious ancestors in earlier enquiry. I have suggested a series of solutions whose ancestry is very evident, but I believe that they are of more than historical interest. The significant juncture I mentioned at the outset is one at which two roads lead in opposite directions: towards and away from physicalism. The former now appears to lead back to reductionism, the latter moves towards hylomorphic personalism; towards a return to form in the philosophy of mind.

Department of Moral Philosophy
University of St Andrews
Fife KY16 9AL
UK
jjh1@st-andrews.ac.uk

IV

MIXING MATTERS

Kit Fine

Abstract
Aristotle raised a puzzle about the possibility of mixing whose
solution is by no means obvious. I here explicate his solution to
the puzzle and attempt to make it plausible within the context of
his thought. Although we now know that his specific views on
mixing were mistaken, his discussion of the topic raises questions
concerning the role of capacities and the relationship of part to
whole that are still of interest.

The topic of mixture plays a central role in Aristotle's metaphysics.[1] For every concrete substance is composed of mixtures
and underlying every substantial change is a process of mixing.
Thus no understanding of substance or of substantial change is
complete without an understanding of mixtures and mixing.
Aristotle's account of mixture may also be of some contemporary
interest. For it depends upon a view, still worthy of attention, of
how dispositions may conflict.

The main text in which mixture is discussed is chapter I.10 of
Generation and Corruption (hereafter *GC*). Aristotle there raises
two puzzles that purport to show that mixing is impossible. The
first, stated at 327a33–327b10, concerns the status of the ingredients as they are mixed. Consider any one of the ingredients that
is to be mixed. Either it continues to exist, once it has been
'mixed', or it does not. If it still exists, then it must have remained
unaltered in the process of mixing and hence cannot properly be
said to have been mixed. But if it no longer exists, then it must
have been destroyed in the process of mixing and so, again,
cannot properly be said to have been mixed.

The other puzzle, stated at 327b31–328a16, concerns the way
the ingredients get divided up as they are mixed. There would
appear to be two alternatives. Under the first, the ingredients are
divided into *pieces*, i.e. into bodies which are further divisible, any

[1] The present paper is a much abridged version of Fine (1995). Many people have
helped me develop the ideas in these two papers; and I am especially indebted to the work
of Bogen (1995) and Code (1995).

piece of one being placed alongside a piece of the other. Under the second, the ingredients are divided into *particles*, i.e., into bodies which are not further divisible, any particle of one being placed alongside a particle of the other. But the first process will not result in what is properly a mixture, for the pieces themselves will not have been mixed. And the second process is an impossibility, for how can a finite body be divided into what are presumably infinitesimal particles?

Aristotle's response to the first puzzle is to draw a distinction between actual and potential existence; 'each of the things which were, before they were mixed, still is, but potentially, and has not been destroyed' (327b2–26). His response to the second puzzle is to maintain that the ingredients accommodate themselves to one another; 'each changes from its own nature in the direction of the dominating one, though it does not become the other but something in between and common to both' (328a27–30). However, it is far from clear what these proposals come to or how they solve the puzzles. What does Aristotle mean here by 'potential' existence? How might the potential existence of the ingredients in the mixture account for their being altered, in the relevant sense, and yet not destroyed? What is the process of mutual accommodation? How does it avoid the dilemma posed by the second puzzle? And why does it result in the potential existence of the ingredients rather than simply in their being destroyed?

The answer to these questions is by no means obvious. Aristotle's view is not at all analogous to the present-day conception of mixing in terms of chemical bonding. A mixture, for him, must be through and through the same (314a20, 328a10). Butter for example, must be the same all the way down; and there is no stage, in its division into parts, at which its property of being butter will be lost. Nor is it his view that mixing is simply a case of two ingredients becoming coincident (as suggested by Sharvy (1983)). Certainly, for him, the ingredients will become coincident in a mixture (for how else could the mixture be through and through the same?). But they do not *simply* become coincident. They interact; and it is through their interaction, that the mixture is formed and coincidence attained. As Aristotle himself puts it at the end of *GC* I.10, 'mixing is the unification of the things mixed resulting from their alteration'.

But if his view is neither atomistic interaction nor non-interactive coincidence, then what is it? How is the desired combination of unification and interaction to be achieved?

In discussing this question, it will be important to distinguish between two rather different aspects of the puzzles, one dynamic and the other static. We may ask what *mixing* is or what *mixture* is. The one concerns the nature of the *process* by which mixtures are formed and relates to what happens over time. The other concerns the nature of the *results* of mixing and relates to what is true at a time. My emphasis, in what follows, is on the static question, although a great deal of interest also attaches to the dynamic question.

1 Accommodation

Let us begin by attempting to understand in what way a mixture is an accommodation of its ingredients.

To fix our ideas, let us suppose that we mix water with air to form 'bubbly'. There is an obvious way in which the bubbly is the result of an accommodation between the water and the air, for it will possess features that are, in an obvious way, a compromise between those of its ingredients. The bubbly will share in the 'lightness' of the air, for example; and the more air there is in the mixture, the lighter the mixture will be (cf. 328b10–14).

But there is a more significant way, for Aristotle, in which the features of a mixture are a compromise between those of the ingredients; not merely the accidental features, but also the formal features, will be the result of a compromise. The form of the bubbly, for example, will be some sort of compromise between the forms of the water and the air.

Moreover, it is plausible to suppose that for Aristotle the accommodation of the form is not simply a *by-product* of the accommodation of the ingredients but is that in which the accommodation of the ingredients consists. After all, he describes the change in the ingredients as a change 'in their nature'; and he is sometimes prepared to talk of the contraries (that compose the elemental forms) as mixing, as if this were somehow more basic than the mixing of the elements themselves (334b16–17).

Can we therefore understand the mixing of two ingredients as simply the result of a compromise in their forms? I think not. It is evident that, for Aristotle, the ingredients from which a mixture is formed are somehow present within it. For if they are not destroyed in the process of mixing, then how could they fail to be present in the resulting mixture? The present account, however, provides no clear justification for this view and hence no clear solution to the puzzle. To be sure, the form of the mixture is a compromise between the forms of the ingredients. But why should that make us think that the ingredients themselves are present in the mixture? Why not say, instead, that the original ingredients have been destroyed and that a new thing, with a compromise form, has emerged in their place?

One might be tempted, at this point, to attribute to Aristotle the view that it is in a somewhat special sense that the elements, or other ingredients, are present in a mixture. Why should he not say that for an element to be present in the mixture is for the mixture to possess the form of that element in a suitably modified manner. Thus for water to be present in the bubbly is for the bubbly to be waterish to some degree; and for some *particular* water to be present in the bubbly is for it to be responsible for the degree to which the bubbly is waterish.

A proposal along these lines is made by Bogen (1995). It does indeed secure a sense in which the ingredients are present in something which might be *thought* to be mixture, but it is not the kind of presence that would guarantee that this something *is* a mixture. After all, it is in much the same sense of 'presence' that we may talk of seeing a father or a mother in a child; for the child is like the father or mother, and the father and mother are respectively responsible for the extent to which the child is like them.[2] But we would not want to say that the father and mother have the kind of presence in the child which would guarantee that the child is a mixture of its parents; and no more should we suppose, under the present account, that the elements have the kind of presence in the putative mixture that would guarantee that it genuinely is a mixture of those elements.

We must dig deeper into the nature of the accommodation of form if we are to see how it might serve to solve the puzzles.

2 The Composition of Form

I believe that the text of *Generation and Corruption*, in which the puzzles are introduced, does not itself provide a clear account of the accommodation of form in mixing and that we must look

---

[2] For the purposes of this example, it is better if we ignore Aristotle's actual views on progeniture!

elsewhere in the Aristotelian corpus, and especially in chapter I.7 of the *Metaphysics*, to discover what he had in mind.

In that chapter, he is concerned with the nature of 'intermediates', i.e. of qualities that lie between two contraries or extremes. The two extremes might be Hot and Cold, for example, and the intermediates would then consist of the various degrees of warmth.

A natural view to take towards a range of contraries and their intermediates is that they merely occupy a sliding scale of qualities of different intensity and that no one contrary or intermediate is more basic than another. But this view, natural as it may be, is not Aristotle's. For him, 'the intermediates must be composed out of the contraries' (1057a18). Thus the contraries are the basic qualities, from which all the other qualities within the given range are formed.

His reasons for holding this view are interesting. He wishes to explain why the transition from one contrary to the other always takes place in the orderly way that it does through the various intermediates and does not jump from cold, let us say, to hot (1057b23–5). His answer is that it is because the intermediates are 'compounded out of the contraries' (1057b23). Thus qualitative change is taken to be a form of quantitative change – for something to become hotter is for it to contain more heat or less cold; and the gradual nature of qualitative change is then explained in terms of the gradual nature of quantitative change.

That this is his view is amply confirmed in his other writings. In *De Sensu*, he assumes that the different colours are combinations of black and white (439b18–440b25), that the 'the intermediate savours arise from the sweet and bitter' (442a13–14), and that 'our conception of the nature of the odours must be analogous to that of the savours' (442b26). In the *Physics*, he proposes a similar view of motion, 'every locomotion ... is either in a circle or a line or mixed; and the two former must be prior to the latter, since they are the elements of which the latter consists' (265a14–16; cf. *De Caelo* I.2, 268b17–20). The formulations of *Generation and Corruption* are also strongly suggestive of this view. For example, at 334b10, he refers to an intermediate between hot and cold as hot-cold or cold-hot, as if it were itself a combination of hot and cold.

Now the form of a mixture, for Aristotle, is a ratio of elements – so much earth, to so much air, to so much fire, to so much water (cf. *Metaphysics* A.10, 993a16–20). This makes it irresistible to suppose, given that an intermediate is a combination of contraries, that the form of a mixture is a like combination of elemental forms. Thus the form of a mixture, for him, is not simply a compromise between the forms of its ingredients, but is actually composed of those forms. The form of the mixture will, in this sense, itself be a mixture of the forms of its ingredients.

But is such a view intelligible? After all, the forms of the elements are themselves combinations of contraries – earth being the combination of cold and dry, air of hot and wet, fire of hot and dry, and water of cold and wet (*GC*, II.3). But this means that the form of bubbly will be composed of hot and wet and of cold and wet, and so the bubbly itself would have to be both hot and cold. And surely this is impossible.

It is true that if hot and cold were straightforward categorical properties (like *feeling* hot or *feeling* cold), then it would be hard to see how both could simultaneously be present in the same object. But the contraries, for Aristotle, are more in the nature of dispositions – hot, for example, is 'that which aggregates things that are of the same kind' and cold is 'that which gathers and aggregates indiscriminately things that are related and things that are not of the same type'. And given that this is so, there is no direct conflict involved in the simultaneous presence of opposed contraries.

But might there not be an indirect conflict? To avoid unnecessary complications that arise from Aristotle's own account of hot and cold, let us suppose that hot is simply the disposition to warm a non-hot body that is placed next to it and that cold is simply the disposition to cool a non-cold body that is placed next to it. Take now a warm body. By hypothesis, it possesses both hot and cold. So when another warm body is placed next to it, that body should be both warmed and cooled, it should become *categorically* warmer and cooler. And this is impossible.

To overcome this second difficulty, we need to be clearer on the connection between a disposition and the dispositional behaviour to which it gives rise. If a body possesses hot, then it will warm an adjacent body as long as it does not also possess cold; and, similarly, if a body possesses cold, then it will cool an adjacent body as long as it does not also possess hot. However, if a body possesses both hot and cold, then the presence of the one disposition will check the dispositional behaviour associated with the other; and, generally, if a body possesses several dispositions, then each may help check or qualify the dispositional behaviour associated with any of the others.

We need to distinguish two forms of dispositional behaviour that may be associated with any given disposition. There is the dispositional behaviour which arises from the unqualified or unchecked presence of the disposition and that which arises from the general presence of the disposition, whether qualified or unqualified. What easily causes confusion between the two is that a disposition may often be *identified* in terms of the first kind of behaviour.[3] Thus hot, in our example, is identified as the disposition to warm adjacent bodies. However, in saying this, we are not saying that a hot body will always warm adjacent bodies, but only that it will warm adjacent bodies when no counter-active dispositions are present. The disposition is identified in terms of its unimpeded operation but the manner of its impeded or qualified operation is left unspecified.

The resolution of our difficulty is now at hand; for once we recognize how the presence of one disposition may modify the operation of another, we see how two dispositions might simultaneously be present in an object even though they would not then both operate in the way they would if the other disposition were absent. It seems to be something like this that Aristotle has in mind at 334b9–16 of *GC*. He writes:

> When one [of hot and cold] exists *simpliciter* in actuality, the other exists in potentiality; when, however, it is not completely so, but hot-cold or cold-hot, because in being mixed things destroy each other's excesses, then what will exist is neither their matter nor either of the contraries existing *simpliciter* in actuality, but something intermediate, which, in so far as it is in potentiality more hot than cold or vice versa, is proportionately twice as hot in potentiality as cold, or three times, or in some other similar way.

Here hot and cold existing '*simpliciter* in actuality' corresponds to their unqualified presence, and their not being completely actual to their qualified presence. Their simultaneous presence in a body is then effected through some sort of accommodation in the potentiality of each contrary (when considered apart from the other).

The present view has radical consequences for the metaphysics of dispositions. To any disposition there corresponds a

---

[3] Even this will not be possible should two dispositions give rise to the same behaviour in an unqualified state but to different behaviour in the presence of other dispositions.

dispositional property, the property of behaving in a way characteristic of objects with that disposition; and it is natural to suppose that there is no significant distinction to be drawn between the two. But this cannot be sensibly maintained under the present view. For consider the dispositional properties corresponding to the dispositions of hot and cold. In order to specify the dispositional behaviour of a body that possesses the disposition of hot, we must distinguish between the case in which it possesses the disposition of hot alone and the case in which it also possesses the disposition of cold. In the former case, it will act in an untempered way in warming neighbouring bodies; while, in the latter case, it will act in a somewhat tempered way. And similarly for the disposition of cold. Thus it will be impossible to specify either dispositional property without bringing in the other disposition; and so it is not clear how we could form a properly grounded conception of the dispositional properties if we were to treat them as identical to the dispositions themselves.

This suggests that we should think of a disposition as a real (categorical) presence in the world, that somehow attaches itself to the object and gives rise to one kind of dispositional behaviour or another, depending upon which other dispositions might also be attached to the body. Of course, the view that dispositions are categorical in nature is not at all uncommon. Armstrong (in Crane (ed.) (1996)) for example, identifies a disposition with a categorical property, such as atomic structure, that underlies the corresponding dispositional behaviour. But, in the present case, we are taking a disposition to be an entity in its own right, not a property, and one, moreover, that can only be identified holistically in terms of the pattern of dispositional behaviour to which it gives rise in conjunction with the other dispositions, and not in terms of some independently identifiable categorical features of the object.

3 Derived Part

We have shown how if one thing results from mixing two other things then the *forms* of the ingredients will be present in the form of the mixture, but not that the *ingredients* themselves will be present. How is this further conclusion to be reached?

Before tackling this question, it will be helpful to consider some analogous questions. Consider the proposition that Socrates is wise and Socrates is Greek. Then the most natural way to analyze this proposition is as the conjunction Ws + Gs of two propositions Ws and Gs, where Ws is the proposition that Socrates is wise and Gs is the proposition that Socrates is Greek. But we might also analyze the proposition as the result of applying the conjunctive property of being a wise Greek to Socrates. Using (W + G) for the conjunctive property, the proposition is then of the form (W + G)s; and the fact that these two analyses are of the same proposition is given by identity:

$$(1) \quad (W + G)s = Ws + Gs.$$

Let us grant that each of these analyses is an analysis of the proposition into *parts*. Then (1) will provide us with two different ways of decomposing the given proposition into parts.

Another case derives from Aristotle's discussion of Hermes and the half-line in the *Metaphysics*. At Δ.7, 1017b8, he claims that 'Hermes is [potentially] in the stone and the half of the line is [potentially] in the line'. We have here a case of one thing being present in another which is much closer to the way in which an ingredient is meant to be present in a mixture. But how might we justify Aristotle's claim that the half-line is *present* in the line and not merely *generable* from the line?

Here is a suggestion. We may take the line to be a hylomorphic compound Lm of a linear form L and of some underlying matter m. This matter is the juxtaposition $m_1 + m_2$ of the parcels of matter m_1 and m_2 corresponding to the two half-lines; and so the line itself is the compound $L(m_1 + m_2)$. But we may also take the line to be the juxtaposition of the two half-lines Lm_1 and Lm_2. Thus, just as in the case of the conjunctive proposition, we will have an identity:

$$(2) \quad L(m_1 + m_2) = Lm_1 + Lm_2$$

that represents two alternative ways of decomposing the line into parts.

I now wish to maintain that a similar account can be given for mixtures. Consider again our bubbly. It is a hylomorphic compound Bm of some matter m and a bubbly form B – where B, as we have seen, is a combination W + A of the form of water and the form of air. But instead of seeing the bubbly as a compound (W + A)m of some matter and a 'mixed' form (W + A), we may also see it as a 'mix' (Wm + Am) of the simple compounds Wm and Am. Thus we will have an identity:

$$(3) \quad (W + A)m = Wm + Am;$$

that represents two different decompositions of the bubbly into parts, one containing the complex form $(W + A)$ as a part and the other containing the two elements Wm and Am as parts.

I do not wish to maintain that Aristotle explicitly sanctions the transition from the one form of decomposition to the other. But it is what his position on mixture seems to require; it appears to be implicit in what he says of Hermes and the line; and, given how natural the transition is, it is not surprising that it should be made without explicit comment. It is therefore not entirely unreasonable to suppose that it is in some such way that he would have wanted to justify the further claim that the ingredients themselves are present in mixture.

We see how the static versions of each of Aristotle's two puzzles can be solved. Since the bubbly $(W + A)m$ admits the alternative decomposition Wm + Am, it becomes clear how the elemental ingredients Wm and Am will also be present in the mixture, though their presence will be qualified in much the same way as their forms. Moreover, since the ingredients Wm and Am possess the common matter m, we see how they can both be present in the mixture without being divided into either pieces or particles. However, the dynamic versions of the puzzles remain. We have not shown how, for Aristotle, the water and air which are in the bubbly might justifiably be taken to be the same as the water and air from which the bubbly was formed or from the water and air which might subsequently be generated from the bubbly. Nor have we shown how one might mix the water and air so thoroughly as to obtain a mixture whose every part contained some of the original water and air.[4] But enough has been said, I hope, to make the interpretation seem plausible and the solution of interest.

Department of Philosophy
New York University
100 Washington Square East
New York
NY 10003
USA
kf14@is4.nyu.edu

---

[4] These, and several other questions, are addressed in the longer paper.

References

Bogen, J. (1995). 'Fire in the Belly: Aristotelian Elements, Organisms, and Chemical Compounds', *Pacific Philosophical Quarterly* 76, nos.3&4, pp.370–404.

Code, A., (1995). 'Potentiality in Aristotle's Science and Metaphysics', *Pacific Philosophical Quarterly* 76, nos. 3&4, pp. 405–418.

Crane, T. (ed.) (1996). *Dispositions: A Debate* (London: Routledge).

Fine, K. (1995). 'Aristotle on Mixture', *Pacific Philosophical Quarterly* 76, nos. 3&4, pp.266–369.

Sharvy, R. (1983). 'Aristotle on Mixtures', *Journal of Philosophy* 80, no. 8, pp.139–457.

Williams, C. J. F. (1982). *Aristotle's 'De Generatione et Corruptione'* (Oxford: Clarendon Press).

V

ON THE UNITY OF COMPOUND THINGS:
LIVING AND NON-LIVING

Joshua Hoffman and Gary S. Rosenkrantz

Abstract
There appear to be at least two kinds of compound physical
substances: compound pieces of matter, which have their parts
essentially, and living organisms, which do not. Examples of the
former are carbon atoms, salt molecules, and pieces of gold; and
examples of the latter are protozoa, trees, and cats. Given that
there are compound entities of these two kinds, and given that
they can be created or destroyed by assembly or disassembly, questions naturally arise about the nature of the causal relations which
unite their parts. In answer to these questions, we first argue that
the parts of a compound piece of matter are connected *via* a relation of dynamic equilibrium of attractive and repulsive forces. We
then argue that the parts of an organic living thing are united in
a different way: they are functionally connected in a broadly
Aristotelian sense which is compatible with an ultimately non-
teleological, naturalistic biology.

I Introduction

This paper is a contribution to the ontology of physical
substances. By a 'physical substance' we mean a *physical object*, and
not a quantity of physical stuff. An important question for an
ontology which includes compound physical substances is the
following: what causal relations unite the parts of such
compound entities? There may appear to be at least four kinds of
compound physical substances, namely, compound pieces of
matter, which have their parts essentially, and artifacts, organic
living things, and inanimate natural formations, which do not.
Examples of these are molecules, ships, cats, and stars, respectively. We shall call a compound piece of matter, e.g., a salt molecule, or a piece of gold, a *mereological compound* for short.

Aristotle's ontology appears to include both mereological
compounds and living organisms. On the other hand, Aristotle
argues that artifacts are ontologically suspect, on the ground that
the essence or form of an artifact, unlike the form of either a

compound piece of matter or a living organism, is not a natural kind.[1] We agree with Aristotle and have argued that any genuine physical substance must have a form which is a natural kind.[2] We also have argued that possessing a form of this kind entails possessing a corresponding essential compositional character. However, a typical inanimate natural formation, for instance, a star, does *not* have such a form, since a star's compositional character is accidental. For example, a star's matter can gradually change from a mixture of hydrogen and helium to carbon. So, our arguments also imply that typical inanimate natural formations are ontologically suspect.[3] However, no such compositional transformations are possible in the case of either a mereological compound or a living organism.

Accordingly, in this paper we shall only ask what causal relations unite the parts of mereological compounds and organic living things, and we will make no similar inquiry about artifacts and typical inanimate natural formations.[4]

There are two extreme positions about what is required for the unity of the parts of a physical compound. According to the first, the parts in question must be literally continuous with one another as well as physically inseparable. This view leads to the conclusion that only true atoms, or simple, fundamental physical objects exist. At the other extreme is the collectionist view that *any* collection of physical parts form a physical substance, no matter how scattered these parts. Both the atomist and collectionist views contradict the commonsense view that there are compound physical substances (such as pieces of wood and cats) which can be created or destroyed by assembly or disassembly. Elsewhere we have defended the commonsense view, insofar as it countenances the existence of both compound pieces of matter and organic living things, and so for the purposes of this paper, we presuppose that both the collectionist and the atomist views are mistaken.[5] Thus, we assume that there exist compound pieces of matter and living organisms, and that they are objects of

---

[1] While Aristotle seems to deny the reality of artifacts, he acknowledges the reality of the underlying pieces of matter. Also note that an artifact's 'existence' is logically dependent upon our beliefs and decisions in a way in which the actual existence of a physical substance belonging to a natural kind is not.

[2] See Joshua Hoffman and Gary S. Rosenkrantz, *Substance: Its Nature and Existence* (London: Routledge, 1997), chap. 5.

[3] *Ibid.*, chap. 5.

[4] *Ibid.*, pp. 150–87.

[5] *Ibid.*, pp. 73–90.

inquiry in the physical and biological sciences, respectively. Accordingly, our project here is to provide analyses of the causal relations which unite the parts of these two kinds of compound things, analyses which will to some extent confirm the common-sense view. In particular, we shall argue that a mereological compound consists of a number of material objects held together by an appropriate unifying causal relation, one whose instantiation by material objects is logically necessary and sufficient for those material objects to compose a mereological compound. We shall also argue for an analysis of a causal relation whose instantiation by physical things is logically necessary and sufficient for those physical things to compose an organism. Such analyses can be used to answer the sceptical charge (made by both atomists and collectionists) that there are no coherent accounts of the causal relations which unite the parts of compound pieces of matter and organic living things as intuitively understood.

These arguments integrate *a priori* conceptual truths with empirical considerations drawn from solid-state physics and evolutionary biology. We shall maintain, in particular, that all of the parts of a mereological compound are connected *via* a relation of dynamic equilibrium of attractive and repulsive forces. In the case of organic living things, we shall contend that all of their parts are functionally connected in a broadly Aristotelian sense which is compatible with an ultimately non-teleological, naturalistic biology.

II The Unity of a Mereological Compound

A compound physical object is one which has parts, parts which can be separated or detached from the object in question. One kind of compound physical object which, we think, belongs to the commonsense ontology is a compound piece of matter (or mereological compound). Henceforth, by a *material object* we shall mean a piece of matter, which could be either a mereological compound or a (non-compound) fundamental material particle. Necessarily, at any time at which a mereological compound exists it has its parts essentially, and therefore cannot undergo mereological change, i.e., cannot gain or lose a part.[6] Because an artifact, an inanimate natural formation, or a living thing is capable

---

[6] To say that an entity, x, has a part, P, *essentially* is to say that (i) x has P as a part, and (ii) it is impossible for x to exist and lack P as a part.

of undergoing mereological change, a mereological compound should be distinguished from a physical object of any of these three kinds, for example, a house, a mountain, or a tree, respectively. As we have noted, a mereological compound consists of a number of material objects held together by an appropriate unifying causal relation, one whose instantiation by a set of material objects is logically necessary and sufficient for those material objects to compose a mereological compound. What is the nature of such a causal relation? In what follows, we shall attempt to answer this question, thereby providing a *principle of unity* for the parts of a mereological compound.

We begin with the assumption that two material objects compose a mereological compound only if they *adhere* to one another in some manner; mere contact (in the ordinary sense) is not enough. But what is the nature of the relevant relation of adherence? Consider, for example, this mereological compound: a piece of solid oak in the shape of a cylinder, six inches long and one quarter inch in diameter. On first thought, it seems relevant that in a wide range of normal circumstances, if we pull or push one half of the cylinder in any direction, then this results in the other half of the cylinder being pulled or pushed in that direction. Yet, it must be admitted that under some normal conditions this result fails to occur. For instance, if a sufficiently powerful force is applied to one half of the cylinder, while the other half of the cylinder is held rigidly in a vise, then this results in the cylinder's snapping in half, with one end remaining at rest in the vise, and the other half moving away from the vise.

But there is second way of thinking about the causal relationship among the cylinder's parts which avoids this difficulty. Roughly speaking, it is that this causal relation's being instantiated by the halves of the cylinder consists in there being a causal relation, R, that holds between these halves, such that either half of the cylinder *may* be pushed or pulled in any direction by pushing or pulling the other half of the cylinder in that direction in virtue of R's holding between the halves in question. (In this context, 'may' means 'it is physically possible that' or 'it is compatible with the laws of nature that', and 'in virtue of' means 'because of'.)

However, this proposal seems subject to another related problem. Even if R holds between the halves of the wooden cylinder, it is clear that R does *not* hold between every pair of parts which compose a mereological compound. For example, consider a short and flimsy piece of cotton thread, T, which is glued with household cement to an object, M, that weighs several tons. We believe that T and M comprise a mereological compound, W. Yet it is clear that if we try to pull M in some direction, d, by pulling T in d with sufficient force, then either T, or the bond between T and M, will break, and in either case, M is not pulled in d by pulling T in d. Thus, it may be wondered whether our second way of thinking about the interrelationship of the wooden cylinder's parts is any more fruitful than the first.

Here is a preliminary sketch of a solution to this problem. To begin with, notice that although, as we have seen, T does *not* bear R to M, T *does* bear such a relationship to some suitably small and lightweight part, P, of M, to which T is glued. That is, P may be detached from the rest of M, and under such conditions, either T or P may be pushed or pulled in any direction by pushing or pulling the other in that direction in virtue of some causal relation that holds between T and P. This suggests that when a number of material objects $P_1...P_n$ compose a mereological compound it need not be true that any two of $P_1...P_n$ bear R to one another, but rather it must be true that each one of $P_1...P_n$ (or a part thereof) bears R to *some* other one of $P_1...P_n$ (or a *part* thereof), yet in such a way that all of $P_1...P_n$ (or *parts* thereof) are connected to one another through a finite number of instances of R. A formal account of the principle of unity for the parts of a mereological compound in terms of this concept of connectedness will be developed and defended later.

But what is the nature of the causal relation R? A hint about how to answer this question was provided by the stoic philosopher Nemesius. As he observed,

> ... there is an inward motion balanced with an outward motion (which accounts for the tension), thus giving rise to the equilibrium of anything.[7]

Following this hint, we analyze the causal relation, R, as follows:

(D1) R is a relation of *dynamic equilibrium* holding between discrete[8] material objects O_1 and O_2=df. (i) R is a relation which holds between O_1 and O_2, and (ii) R is necessarily such

---

[7] Quoted in *Greek and Roman Philosophy after Aristotle*, ed. J. Saunders (New York: The Free Press, 1966), p. 86.

[8] To say that two entities are *discrete* is to say that they have no part (proper or improper) in common.

that, for any x and y, R holds between x and y if and only if (a) there are attractive forces between x and y, and (b) there are repulsive forces between x and y, and (iii) the attractive forces of (ii)(a) and the repulsive forces of (ii)(b) are in equilibrium.

Metaphorically speaking, any relation of dynamic equilibrium holding between material objects O_1 and O_2 composing an object must balance the elements of 'love' and 'hate' between O_1 and O_2.[9] If an object composed of O_1 and O_2 were to lose the attractive elements, while retaining the repulsive elements, then that object would be apt to disintegrate, and if an object composed of O_1 and O_2 were to lose the repulsive elements, while retaining the attractive elements, then that object would be apt to collapse into a zero-dimensional entity lacking parts altogether. (This appears to be a necessary truth knowable *a priori*.) Thus, it seems that the characteristic stability of a non-basic material object could only result from a balance of the elements of 'love' and 'hate' between its parts.

As we have defined the notion of a relation of dynamic equilibrium, some such relations can be weak, some strong, and some of intermediate strength. In analyzing the unifying causal relation that holds among a set of parts which compose a mereological compound we aim to identify what we may call an *adherence relation*, that is, a relation of dynamic equilibrium of the right strength. The notion of a relation of dynamic equilibrium which we have defined in (D1) is a *technical* one. We shall utilize this technical notion in our explication of the causal relation which unites parts that compose a mereological compound. The relation of dynamic equilibrium in question is not to be confused with the yet-to-be defined causal relation or with any of the other, more intuitive, relations of adhesion, bonding, attachment, fastening, or the like.

According to currently accepted scientific theory, the adherence relation instantiated by parts that compose an actual mereological compound results from an equilibrium of attractive and repulsive forces of certain kinds among those parts. The particular nature of such an adherence relation is an empirical question to be decided by scientific investigation of the mereological compound in question. For example, it has been discovered that

---

[9] The metaphor of 'love' and 'hate' is inspired by the doctrine of the presocratic philosopher, Empedocles, who believed that all natural processes are due to the operation of these two opposing influences. See Jonathan Barnes, *Early Greek Philosophy* (London: Penguin Books, 1987), pp. 161–201.

there is a relatively long-range attractive force between atoms or molecules as well as a relatively short-range repulsive force which comes into play when the atoms or molecules are close to one another. Current scientific theory implies that an equilibrium must obtain at some middle distance at which the net force is zero.

What does physics have to say about the nature of these forces? Physics recognizes four fundamental forces, and if material objects are attached to one another, by gluing, fastening, linking, interlocking, fusing, and so on, then this attachment can ultimately be explained in terms of one or more of these four forces.[10] These four fundamental forces are: (i) gravitational attraction, (ii) the electromagnetic force, manifested in various kinds of chemical bonds and magnetic forces, (iii) the strong force, which is stronger than any other known force, and (iv) the weak force, which affects elementary particles and causes some cases of particle decay, nuclear beta decay, and the ejection and absorption of neutrinos. On any intuitive conception of bonding, the weak force is too feeble to bond objects, and likewise for gravitational forces unless very large masses are involved. In contrast, the strong force is responsible for binding neutrons and protons in the atomic nucleus. Finally, the forces between atoms and molecules are electromagnetic in nature, and include the forces associated with ionic bonds, covalent bonds, Van der Waals forces, repulsive forces, and metallic bonds.

Thus, typically the parts of mereological compounds are held together in virtue of the strong force (which operates only at the subatomic level) and the electromagnetic force (which operates at the interatomic and intermolecular levels).

It seems that if two objects x and y physically bond with one another to form a mereological compound at a time t, then at t there must be a definite distance d such that if x were farther than d from y at t, then x and y would not bond with one another. But, in most cases physics implies that x and y are at a positive distance from one another because of repulsive forces between fundamental particles. Moreover, physics implies that there is a precise positive distance (or at least a definite spatial region) at which (or within which) the attractive forces which bind x and y together and the

---

[10] A caveat is necessary here. Recently, physicists have proposed theories that recognize fewer than the four fundamental forces we have mentioned, attempting to reduce some of them to others or to some new force such as the 'electroweak' force. These theories remain controversial.

repulsive forces which keep x and y apart come into balance or equilibrium, and it would be plausible to identify d with this distance (or with the maximum width of the region in question). Given the findings of physics, we shall understand the attachment or bonding of two pieces of matter x and y, or the bonding of a surface or edge of x to a surface or edge of y, in such a way that it is compatible with, but does not require, x's being at a zero distance from y.

We can now provide an account of the principle of unity for the parts of a mereological compound. The first step is to construct a suitable technical conception of *joining* between material objects in terms of the notion of a relation of dynamic equilibrium and other ideas presented earlier.

(D2) Discrete material objects x and y are joined at a time t =df. at t, there is a relation of dynamic equilibrium, E, holding between x and y such that for any direction, d, it is both (i) physically possible that x is pulled or pushed in direction d thereby pulling or pushing y in direction d in virtue of E's holding between x and y, and (ii) physically possible that y is pulled or pushed in direction d thereby pulling or pushing x in direction d in virtue of E's holding between x and y.

For example, consider the right and left halves of our wooden cylinder. Based upon our earlier discussion of this example, it is clear that (D2) implies that these two halves are joined. That is, these two halves are an x and a y that meet conditions (i) and (ii) of (D2). In contrast, the wooden cylinder, and an inclined plane upon which it rolls downward, are material objects which are not joined, they are an x and a y that meet neither condition (i) nor (ii) of (D2). Nor is the cylinder joined to the Earth, since in that case only *one* of the two conditions set forth in (D2) is satisfied: although it is physically possible to pull or push the Earth in any direction thereby pulling or pushing the cylinder in that direction in virtue of the forces which hold between the Earth and the cylinder, it is not physically possible to pull or push the cylinder in any direction thereby pulling or pushing the Earth in that direction in virtue of those forces. Similarly, a piece of flimsy cotton thread that is glued to a massive object weighing several tons is not joined to that massive object, because just one of the two conditions set forward in (D2) is met: while it is physically possible to pull or push the massive object in any direction thereby pulling or pushing the piece of thread in that direction in virtue of the forces which hold between the massive object and the piece of thread, it is not physically possible to pull or push the piece of thread in any direction thereby pulling or pushing the massive object in that direction in virtue of those forces. Since, intuitively, the piece of thread is attached to the massive object, thereby forming a mereological compound, the joining relation specified in (D2) cannot be identified with the relation commonly thought to attach one part of a material object to another. The latter relation is transitive, whereas the joining relation specified in (D2) is not. Finally, suppose that a nut-shaped piece of iron is threaded onto a bolt-shaped piece of iron, are they joined or not? The answer depends upon the exact circumstances. On the one hand, suppose that the nut-shaped piece of iron is loose, and that turning it in some direction doesn't cause the bolt-shaped piece of iron to turn in that direction. In that case, at most one of the two conditions in (D2) is satisfied, and therefore the nut and the bolt are not joined. On the other hand, suppose that the nut-shaped piece of iron has been tightened up, so that by turning the nut-shaped piece of iron one thereby turns the bolt-shaped piece of iron, and vice versa. If so, then both of the conditions in (D2) are satisfied, and the nut-shaped piece of iron and the bolt-shaped piece of iron are joined.

By making use of the concept of joining defined in (D2), and the standard formal notion of connectedness, we can define the following notion of material objects $P_1...P_n$ being connected *via* the joining relation (or *joined and connected* for short).

(D3) Discrete material objects $P_1...P_n$ are connected *via* the joining relation at a time t =df. at t, for any two of $P_1...P_n$, P_x and P_y, there is some finite number of joinings, each of which joins one of $P_1...P_n$ (or a part thereof) to another one of $P_1...P_n$ (or a part thereof), by which a path can be traced from P_x (or a part thereof) to P_y (or a part thereof).[11]

---

[11] Note that while the top third and the bottom third of a wooden block are connected via the joining relation, they are not joined, despite the fact there is some sort of dynamic equilibrium of gravitational and other forces between them, and they can be pushed and pulled together. For our analysis requires more than this in order for two pieces of matter to be joined, namely, that their *attractive* and *repulsive* forces are in a state of dynamic equilibrium, S, such that it is physically possible for them to be pushed and pulled together *in virtue of S*. This implies that S is a bond of sufficient strength. But the top third and the bottom third of the wooden block do not satisfy this requirement: gravitational forces, although long-range, are far too weak for joining (unless of course huge masses are involved), and thus normally cannot come into a sufficiently robust balance with the powerful repulsive forces of objects; while these repulsive forces are extremely short-range, and hence cannot come into a sufficiently robust balance with any strong attractive forces at a distance even as small as 1/3 of the height of a small wooden block.

(D3) is an analysis of a causal relation which unites the parts of a mereological compound. The promised principle of unity for the parts of a mereological compound can now be expressed as the following necessary equivalence.

(P_{MC}) (Discrete material objects $P_1...P_n$ compose a mereological compound at a time t) $\Leftrightarrow$ (at t, $P_1...P_n$ are connected *via* the joining relation).

In the light of our earlier explanations, we can see that (P_{MC}) has the desirable implication that each of the following pairs of material things composes a mereological compound: the right and left half halves of our wooden cylinder, a bolt-shaped piece of iron and a nut-shaped piece of iron which is tightened on the bolt-shaped piece of iron, and a piece of flimsy cotton thread and a very heavy object to which it is glued. For in each of these cases, the pair of objects in question satisfies (D3), i.e., they (or some parts of them) are connected *via* the joining relation, even though in the third case they fail to satisfy (D2), i.e., they are not joined. It is also clear, given our previous discussions, that (P_{MC}) has the welcome implication that the following pairs of entities are *not* united into a mereological compound: the wooden cylinder and the inclined plane that it is rolling down, the wooden cylinder and the Earth, and the bolt-shaped piece of iron and the nut-shaped piece of iron which turns freely on the bolt-shaped piece of iron. Because (P_{MC}) has the correct implications in these cases, and in many other similar ones that the reader is invited to imagine, (D3) seems to provide a satisfactory analysis of the causal relation which is intuitively thought to unite the parts of a mereological compound. Finally, (P_{MC}) clarifies the sense in which a mereological compound or compound piece of matter is *solid* or *stable*, unlike typical liquids and gases.[12]

As we have stated, in our view it is an *a priori* truth that stability

---

[12] All material substances which do not perceptibly flow are commonly regarded as *solids*, but between an ordinary solid and an ordinary liquid there are many intermediate forms, for instance, viscous solids, semi-solids, and viscous liquids. We have argued that typical solids, unlike typical liquids, are mereological compounds. But given the gradations that exist between typical solids and typical liquids, can a precise distinction be drawn between mereological compounds and masses of atoms or molecules which are not mereological compounds? We believe that such a distinction can be drawn. After all, for *any* material objects $P_1...P_n$, (D1), (D2), (D3), and (P_{MC}) together provide a precise and determinate answer as to whether or not $P_1...P_n$ are united into a mereological compound. In other words, there is always a fact of the matter as to whether or not $P_1...P_n$ are joined and connected at some time. Determining in a particular case whether or not

entails a dynamic equilibrium of the specified kind. This view might be questioned as follows. Consider, for example, a chain-like structure consisting of (fairly tightly fitting) links extending in three orthogonal directions. Such an entity would move as a unitary whole, though at rest, there would be no strong attractive forces between the links keeping them from moving apart, and no strong repulsive forces between them making them tend to move apart. That is, there would not be a 'dynamic equilibrium' between the links of the sort we require. The difference between such a chain-like structure and the sort of structure we require for stability is that in the former, the relevant forces only come into operation shortly after various parts of the object are pushed or pulled, so that there is some 'give' between these parts, whereas in the latter, the forces are constantly in operation, so that there is no 'give' between those parts. However, it is possible for there to be a macroscopic object whose microstructure is a chain-like structure of the sort described. And it is possible for our observations of such an object's macroscopic behavior when it is pushed or pulled to give us every reason to believe that it is a paradigm case of a 'solid' object. It might be inferred from this that stability does *not* entail a dynamic equilibrium of the sort we have described.

We answer this objection in two ways. First, if we were able to see (what are in fact) microscopic objects, then the structural difference between the two types of objects under discussion *would* result in observable differences in the behavior of each type of object, when various of their parts were pushed or pulled. That is, we would observe some 'give' in one case and not in the other. Since the principle of unity for the parts of a *material* substance cannot be logically dependent on the resolving power of the sense-organs of human (or other) observers, no reason has been provided to doubt that stability entails a dynamic equilibrium of the sort we require. Second, it is clear that a *macroscopic* chain-link structure of an ordinary sort does not display the

---

some $P_1...P_n$ are joined and connected at a particular time is an empirical question that is to be decided by scientific means. Of course, we readily admit that there might be an instance of some form of matter intermediate between typical solids and typical liquids with respect to which making such a determination is a daunting task. However, although we admit that in some cases there might be *empirical* difficulties in ascertaining whether or not certain objects are united into a mereological compound, no reason has yet surfaced for thinking that there is any *conceptual* difficulty in drawing a precise distinction between those masses of atoms and molecules which are so united and those which are not.

characteristic stability of a 'solid' object. Thus, it is intuitive that an ordinary chain is not such an object. This is true as well of a corresponding microscopic chain. Hence, in the case of a macroscopic object with a chain-link microstructure, there is a set of non-solid parts, i.e., microscopic chains, which compose that macroscopic object. Yet, it seems that if an object is composed of parts which are not solid, then it itself is not solid.

Thus, in the light of the foregoing two replies, it appears that a macroscopic object with a chain-link structure is not 'solid'. We conclude that the objection under discussion does not succeed.

Finally, it might be objected that (P_{MC}) is viciously circular as an analysis of the unity of a mereological compound. But we do not claim either that (P_{MC}) is a definition, or that it provides such an analysis. We only claim that (P_{MC}) is a necessary bi-conditional, in contrast to an analysis, which is an *explanatory* necessary bi-conditional. But we do claim that in (D3) we have analyzed the corresponding causal relation. Parallel remarks apply to the principle of organization for the parts of an organic living thing we shall provide in the next section.

III The Unity of a Living Thing

Our analysis of the causal relation which unites the parts of a living thing is intended only to cover those organisms which have a composition or structure of a certain kind, one which entails having information-encoding, carbon-based macromolecules together with water molecules as parts. Examples of such organisms are tigers, trees, paramecia, bacteria, algae, and mushrooms. Necessarily, something is a living *organism* only if it is an organic living entity which is not a *part* of another organic living entity. On the other hand, it seems that a nerve-cell, a brain, and a central nervous system are organic living entities which typically *are* parts of another organic living entity, e.g., a tiger. Thus, *organic living parts* of these kinds typically do not qualify as organisms.[13]

As we have argued, material objects $P_1...P_n$ being joined and connected is logically necessary and sufficient for $P_1...P_n$ to compose a mereological compound. Yet, a set of atoms or

---

[13] This leaves open the possibility that there are organic living entities which are neither organisms nor parts of organisms. It can be argued that a malignant cell, a living heart which is detached from an organism, or cells kept alive in a tissue culture are such organic living entities.

molecules composing a functioning organism, whether unicellular or multicellular, are *not* joined and connected. This is implied by the following two facts. First, any *functioning* organism is in large measure composed of organic solids and liquid water intermingled. Second, since liquid water consists of molecules which are not joined and connected, liquid water cannot be joined and connected to a surrounding container, for example, a cell wall or membrane. Thus, the principle of organization for the parts of an organism should *not* require that the parts which compose an organism be joined and connected. This fact serves to sharply distinguish the unity of parts of an organism from that of the parts of a mereological compound. It is clear from the fact that all or most living things are in part liquid, that the unity of their parts requires instead that the parts which compose an organism be interconnected *via* some causal relation other than that of being joined and connected. Thus, the central question confronting us concerns the nature of this other causal relation.

Evidently, an organism's parts function in numerous ways to facilitate its life-processes. We shall argue that the causal unity of the parts of an organism can be analyzed in terms of their *functional connectedness*. The functions of such parts fall into two categories: *b-functions* and *n-functions*. A b-function is a basic biological activity of a part of an organism, and an n-function is a naturally selected biological activity of a part of an organism. Biological evolution and natural selection could not occur unless the first organisms had parts which possessed b-functions.

The notion of a b-function can be clarified with the following device. This device consists in using a comprehensive set of conditions, *S*, which is logically sufficient for organic life, and includes all of the fundamental activities of organic life which are logically necessary for organic life. It is possible to pick out such a set of conditions, *S*, because there is a family of fundamental, causally interrelated activities of organic life (together with a structure for organic life) without a general capacity for which (or without the presence of which) species of organic life could not exist. This family consists of the activities of absorption, excretion, metabolism, growth, reproduction, and (perhaps) biosynthesis, in conjunction with a cellular structure. Some of these fundamental biological factors seem to be *a priori* general preconditions for the existence of organic life, e.g., absorption, excretion, growth, and reproduction. Others have been *empirically* discovered, e.g., cellular structure, metabolism, and biosynthesis.

We are now prepared to specify the set, S, which plausibly includes all of the fundamental conditions for organic life.

(D4) The elements of S are the following eight conditions: Where x is a persisting organism, (i) x has parts which are m-molecules, that is, organic macromolecules of repeated units which have a high capacity for selective reactions with other similar molecules, (ii) x has a layer or membrane made of m-molecules whose limit is x's exterior surface, (iii) x absorbs and excretes through this layer or membrane, (iv) x metabolizes m-molecules, (v) x grows through an increase in the number of m-molecules that compose it, (vi) x synthesizes m-molecular parts of x by means of m-molecular parts of x copying themselves, (vii) x reproduces, either by means of x's m-molecular parts copying themselves, or by means another, more basic, process, (viii) x's absorbing and excreting causally contribute to x's metabolizing m-molecules; these jointly causally contribute to x's biosynthesizing m-molecules; these together causally contribute to x's growing and reproducing by means of the addition or copying of m-molecules; and x's growing causally contributes to x's absorbing, excreting, metabolizing, biosynthesizing, and reproducing.

In utilizing (D4), we understand the notion of *a condition's figuring in (D4)* in such a way that if a conjunction's contributing to some result figures in (D4), then the individual contribution of each conjunct figures in (D4) as well. Although we maintain that (D4) is a logically *sufficient* condition for organic life which includes all of an organism's fundamental biological activities, we do *not* claim that having a capacity to engage in *all* of the activities which figure in (D4) is a logically *necessary* condition for organic life.

We are now in a position to elucidate the notion of a b-function of a proper part of an organism. A b-function of a proper part, p, of an organism is either an activity of p's engaging in, or an activity of p's causally contributing to, one or more fundamental biological processes of the sort which figure in conditions (iii)–(vii) of (D4). We elucidate the concept of an n-function as follows:

(D5) $\emptyset$-ing is an n-function had by a proper part, P, of an organism x =df. P is a proper part of x such that: (a) P has the capacity to $\emptyset$, and (b) the trait, having a proper part with the capacity to $\emptyset$, is either naturally selected for x, or naturally selected for one or more ancestors of x, from whom x inherited this trait via some line of descent.

For example, pumping blood is an n-function of a human's heart, digesting food is an n-function of a human's stomach, oxygenating blood is an n-function of a human lung, and so on.[14] Henceforth, by a function of a proper part of an organism we mean either a b-function or an n-function of such a part.[15]

Another, related, notion that we will employ stands in some need of explanation. This is the notion of *the degree to which an organism's life-processes or microstructure are natural*, with *maximal naturalness* as a possible limiting case. To say that an organism's life-processes are maximally natural, or that an organism's microstructure is maximally natural, is to say that they are as natural as they could be, or, in common parlance, 'that they are as nature intended them to be'.

The notions of the degree of naturalness of an organism's life-processes or microstructure presuppose the relational notions of *x's life-processes or microstructure being less natural than y's*. These relational notions are asymmetric, transitive, and irreflexive, and can be illustrated by the following examples. All other things being equal, with respect to life-processes or microstructure, those of a man with a heart transplant are less natural than those of a man without one; those of a man with both a heart transplant and a kidney transplant are less natural than a those of a man with only a heart transplant; those of a man with a liver transplant are less natural than those of a man with a corneal transplant; those of a man with an artificial heart are less natural than those of a man with an artificial ankle-joint; those of a man with an artificial heart are less natural than those of a man with a heart transplant; and those of a man with a heart transplant from a distant relative are less natural than those of a man with a heart transplant from an identical twin.

---

[14] It appears that parts of living organisms have natural functions in the sense of being naturally *for* certain activities, e.g., it appears that hearts are naturally for pumping blood. As we have argued elsewhere, any natural function of this kind can be reduced to an n-function. Aristotle accepts the existence of such biological natural functions, but he would reject our reductionist analysis of them. See Hoffman and Rosenkrantz, *Substance: Its Nature and Existence*, pp. 91–118.

[15] It should be noted that a function may consist of a conjunction of other functions.

Since there are relatively clear relational notions of x's life-processes (or x's microstructure) being less natural than y's life-processes (or y's microstructure), there must be intelligible notions of the degree to which x's life-processes (or x's microstructure) are (is) natural. Generalizing from the foregoing examples, we define the latter notions as follows:

> (D6) x's life-processes (or x's microstructure) are (is) *natural* to the degree that x's life-processes (x's microstructure) conform(s) to the information implicit (at x's first moment of existence) in x's hereditary make-up.

The original hereditary nature of an organism can be identified with an attribute whose content specifies a microstructural 'design' for that organism. (D6) presupposes that for every organism there must be an attribute of this kind, and that instructions for implementing the specifications in question are coded in the organism's original hereditary make-up, that is, in one or more organic macromolecules. The assumption that there are such attributes or *microstructural hereditary blueprints* is both plausible and compatible with current ideas in biology. A 'blueprint' of this kind incorporates a *range* of structural specifications, including the permitted tolerances and allowances for an organism's functional parts. In other words, it includes the range of variation permitted in maintaining a specified dimension when a functional part is generated, and the allowed dimensional differences for functional parts having directly interrelated activities. This includes, for example, the range of sizes from minimum to maximum for the inner diameter of certain blood vessels, the greatest allowable difference in size between the heart and the kidneys, and so on. Implicit in such a 'blueprint' is a parallel range of specifications pertaining to the character and interrelationship of an organism's life-processes at a microstructural level. In other words, a microstructural hereditary blueprint is equivalent to an indefinitely long disjunction of non-disjunctive microstructural attributes, a property of the form 'P_1 or P_2 or P_3 or P_4 or ...', where the first disjunct resembles the second, the second resembles the third, the third resembles the fourth, and so on. Thus, an organism's (O's) possession of a microstructural hereditary blueprint is compatible with the fact that the way in which O's heredity or genes are expressed in O's microstructure or life-processes is partly dependent upon environmental conditions.[16]

By utilizing the notion of a microstructural hereditary blueprint, we can now say that x's life-processes or x's microstructure is *natural* to the degree that it conforms to the information implicit in x's microstructural hereditary blueprint. We plan to employ both the notion of a function of a part of an organism, and the notion of the degree to which an organism's life-processes are natural, to provide a satisfactory principle of organization for the parts of an organism.

It is necessary for any organism to have one or more *vital* parts. For example, typically, a human being has vital organs such as a brain and a heart. And it seems that organ-*systems* such as the nervous, cardiovascular, digestive, respiratory, and excretory systems are vital parts of an ordinary human being. Organs, or organ-systems, of these kinds have functions, e.g., pumping blood, digesting food, oxygenating blood, and so forth. In common parlance, functions of this kind are also said to be vital.

The notion of *the degree of naturalness of an organism's (O's) life-processes* can be used to provide an account of the concept of a vital part. As a first step towards the account in question, we observe that v is a vital part of O just in case v is a proper part of O, and there is a function, f, such that: if O's life continues much longer, then O's life must be sustained by v's performing f, *unless* there is a proxy, v^*, which comes to perform f, in place of, or in addition to, v. For example, v^* might be a transplant, an artificial organ, a vital organ of another organism which sustains O's life via some unnatural connection, or an artificial life-support machine. But v^*'s coming to perform, or performing, f necessarily involves an artificial or unnatural aspect or element which is *not* implicit in O's microstructural hereditary blueprint. Thus, v^*'s coming to perform, or performing, f entails that the degree of naturalness of O's life-processes does *not* remain constant. Therefore, the concept of a vital part can be understood as follows:

(D7) v is a vital part of an organism O at a time t =df. (i) v is a proper part of O at t, and (ii) for some time t', later than t, but

---

[16] A related notion is that of a *norm of reaction* for an organism, O, which may be thought of as the range of phenotypes (or body-types) generable by O's genotype (or hereditary-type) in the environmental conditions in which organisms with O's genotype (or hereditary-type) can exist.

not so much later than t that O could not live from t until t', there is a function, f, such that so long as the degree of naturalness of O's life-processes remains constant, O's life-processes continuing from t until t' entails that O's life-processes are sustained by v's performing f at some time t^* ($t \leq t^* < t'$).[17]

Note that (D7) employs the standard modal concept of broadly logical or *metaphysical entailment*, and the ordinary or intuitive notion of a *sustaining cause*, a notion which we shall not attempt to analyze. As is well known, the difficulties involved in providing a philosophical analysis of such an ordinary or intuitive causal concept are formidable.[18] This should not and does not prevent scientists and philosophers from usefully employing such ordinary causal concepts.

In addition to having one or more vital parts, it appears to be necessary for an organism to have *non-vital* parts, examples of which are an eye, an ear, a single water molecule, and so forth. Typically, parts of this kind perform non-vital functions, e.g., inputting visual data, inputting auditory data, engaging in activities which causally contribute to fundamental biological processes, and so on.

Moreover, as Aristotle thought, there is a sense in which organic living, or functional, parts of an organism may jointly act as a unitary functional part, which part may be vital or non-vital. For example, specialized living organelles and other functional items, e.g., mitochondria, a nucleus, Golgi bodies, a cell membrane, and so on, may compose a living cell with a specialized function, such as a lung cell; specialized living cells and other functional items, e.g., lung cells and intracellular materials, may compose a living organ, such as a lung, with a specialized function, e.g., inhaling air; and specialized living organs and other functional items, e.g., lungs, nostrils, and so forth, may compose a living organ-system, such as a respiratory system, with a specialized function, e.g., oxygenating blood. Parallel remarks apply to the composition of other organ systems, e.g., the nervous, cardiovascular, digestive, and excretory systems. It

---

[17] By existentially quantifying over times, (D7) allows the length of time from t until t' to vary from one case of a vital part to another. This is a desirable feature: although in typical cases the heart and the liver are both vital organs, the loss of heart-function ordinarily results in death much more quickly than the loss of liver-function.

[18] Nevertheless, at least this much can be said about the nature of a sustaining cause: an event E_1 sustains an event E_2 only if event E_1 is causally necessary and sufficient in the circumstances for event E_2.

appears that joint activities of the aforementioned kinds are a result of natural selection. Thus, it seems that the living and functional items which compose the relevant cells, organs, and organ-systems *jointly* have an n-function. Moreover, it is intuitively plausible that specialized cells, organs, and organ-systems of the kinds in question are organic living entities. Thus, we are prepared to accept the following principle.

(D8) Necessarily, if $P_1...P_n$ are organic living or functional proper parts of an organism, and at least one of $P_1...P_n$ is an organic living entity, and $P_1...P_n$ have the n-function of $\emptyset$-ing, then $P_1...P_n$ compose an organic living entity, x, that has the n-function of $\emptyset$-ing.

Let us summarize some of the important implications of the foregoing discussion. First, specialized organ-systems, organs, cells of multicellular organisms, and subcellular organelles (at least in some cases) are *organic living parts* of organisms. Thus, an organ-system, organ, cell, or organelle of this kind qualifies as an *organic living entity* for the purposes of the definitions which follow. Second, organic living parts of the foregoing kinds typically have n-functions.

However, since an organism cannot be a proper part of an organic living entity, and since organ-systems, organs, cells of multicellular organisms, and some organelles *are* or *can be* organic living proper parts of an organism, such organic living proper parts, of course, do not qualify as full-fledged *organisms*. This point should be kept in mind in the discussions which follow.

By using the ideas of a vital part and of parts which have a joint n-function, we can sketch the outlines of a promising strategy for providing a principle of organization for the parts of an organism. To begin with, further reflection upon the notion of a vital part reveals that some vital parts have a more central role to play in the unification or organization of an organism's parts than others. Both the heart and the central nervous system are vital parts of a typical human being. Thus, in typical cases the central nervous system's functional activities *sustain* the heart's functional activities, and *vice versa*. But modern biology has discovered that in these cases the central nervous system's functional activities *regulate* or *control* the functional activities of the heart, but *not vice versa*. This seems to have been denied in ancient times by Aristotle. He apparently thought that the heart is the seat of centralized control, and that the brain's activities are controlled by the heart's.[19] Aristotle suggests that no animal has ever been born without a heart,[20] and that when a 'monster' is born we can determine whether we have *one* creature with supernumerary organs or Siamese *twins* by seeing whether there is one heart or two. As Aristotle puts it:

> We must decide whether the monstrous animal is one or is composed of several grown together by considering the vital principle; thus, if the heart is a part of such a kind then that which has one heart will be one animal, the multiplied parts being mere outgrowths, but those which have more than one heart will be two animals grown together through their embryos having been confused.[21]

The principle of organization for the parts of an organism which we will provide confirms the central thrust of this Aristotelian view, though, of course, it is the primitive central nervous system, or notochord-mesoderm, and not the heart, that is the regulative or controlling vital part in question.

It is plausible to suppose that a regulative vital part plays a more central role in the organization of an organism's parts than a non-regulative vital part. For example, it seems that a human's central nervous system plays a more prominent role in organizing a human's parts than does a human's heart. The principle of organization for the parts of an organism which we will defend reflects this distinction between regulative and non-regulative vital parts.

We are now in a position to set forth the following idea as a promising basis for such a principle of organization. According to this idea, if x is a part of an organism, O, and e is any life-process or functional activity of x, then so long as the degree of naturalness of O's life-processes remains constant, e's continuing entails that there is a vital part, v, of O such that e is regulated by the functional activity of v. In this sense, there is at least one vital part, v, of O such that: the life-processes or functional activities of the organic living or functional parts of O are subordinate to v's functional activities. It seems that organic living or functional

---

[19] *Parts of Animals*, trans. W. Ogle, in Jonathan Barnes (ed.), *The Complete Works of Aristotle*, 2 vols. (Princeton: Princeton University Press, 1984), 1:1016, 1022, and 1037–9.

[20] *Generation of Animals*, trans. A. Platt, in *The Complete Works of Aristotle*, 1:1193.

[21] *Ibid.*, p.1196.

entities compose O if and only if these entities are connected in this way. Hence, it appears that there is a sense in which all of O's organic living or functional parts are *united* in virtue of being so connected.

Let us further explore the idea that an organism must have a vital part which regulates or controls that organism's life-processes.[22] We will then define a technical concept of what it is for an organic living or functional entity to be functionally subordinate to such a vital regulative part. This technical concept will play a central role in the principle of organization for the parts of an organism which we will propose.

It is in the nature of an organism to be self-sustaining and self-regulating: any organism must have some vital part whose functional activities *regulate* or *control* the life-processes or functional activities of the parts of that organism. In all known cases, the regulation or control of the life-processes of the parts of an organism is accomplished by means of the activities of a system of biological parts which jointly have an n-function, and this system may vary in its degree of centralization from one kind of organic living thing to another.

Animals appear to have a highly centralized regulatory system. Thus, an adult vertebrate seems to regulate its life-processes by means of the activities of a highly centralized system consisting of its brain and spinal cord, i.e., the central nervous system.[23] On the other hand, a mature plant appears to regulate its life-processes by means of the activities of a rather diffuse or decentralized system.[24] For instance, a typical mature plant, P, may have a regulatory system consisting of P's roots, stem, and leaves. Although this regulatory system is decentralized, it cannot be identified with P as a whole. In particular, P's roots, stem, and leaves comprise much, though not *all*, of P. P also has the water and sugar molecules in its sap as parts, molecules which are discrete from P's roots, stems, and leaves.

A eukaryotic single-celled organism seems to have a highly

---

[22] Whenever we say that an *object, x,* regulates, controls, causally contributes to, or sustains, processes or activities of an object, *y,* this is shorthand for saying that *processes* or *activities* of *x* regulate, control, causally contribute to, or sustain, processes or activities of *y.*

[23] Of course, the nervous system as a whole, a system consisting of the central nervous system together with the peripheral nerves which branch out from it, may also be said to regulate these life-functions.

[24] But at its inception a plant consists of single cell with a centralized regulatory system, namely, its nucleus.

centralized regulatory system, i.e., its nucleus, whereas a prokaryotic single-celled organism appears to have a centralized regulatory system involving its DNA and messenger RNA molecules.

In the light of the foregoing discussion, it seems that there could not be an organism which does not have a *vital proper part* which regulates or controls its life-processes. It appears that even the simplest possible organism, i.e., a first living thing, has such a vital proper part. Since it has both an organic macromolecule and water as parts, and its life-processes are regulated or controlled by information encoded in that macromolecule, its regulatory system is a proper part of itself. We conclude that, necessarily, an organism has a vital regulative proper part. Let us call a part of this kind a *master-part.*

It might be objected that it is not an *a priori* necessary truth that a living organism has such a master-part. Our response is that it is an *a posteriori* necessary truth that a living organism has a master-part. After all, in the relevant sense, *living organism* is a natural kind of physical substance which figures in scientific laws,[25] and the nature of living organisms is an object of empirical investigation in the biological sciences. In particular, it is an *a posteriori* discovery that necessarily, any such living organism has a certain compositional or structural essence, one that includes information-encoding, carbon-based macromolecules and water molecules.[26] Thus, it is our position that there are *a posteriori* necessities about such living things which can be inferred from empirical discoveries in biology and metaphysical premises.[27] If we are right, then these *a posteriori* necessities include the fact that

[25] Observe that necessarily, the property of being a living organism is essential to whatever instantiates it, as seems to be required if *living organism* is to qualify as a natural kind of physical substance. Moreover, a natural kind of compound physical substance must supervene upon structural and compositional attributes. This further requirement for being such a natural kind is also satisfied by *living organism*: necessarily, whatever is compositionally and structurally indistinguishable from a living organism is a living organism.

[26] The view that there are *a posteriori* necessities concerning the compositional or structural essences of entities belonging to various natural kinds has had numerous defenders in recent years. For example, see Saul Kripke's 'Naming and Necessity', in *Semantics of Natural Language*, D. Davidson and G. Harman (eds.), (Dordrecht: Reidel, 1972), pp. 253–355 (also *Naming and Necessity* (Oxford: Blackwell, 1980)). Cf. Hilary Putnam, 'The Meaning of Meaning', in *Minnesota Studies in the Philosophy of Science VII: Language, Mind, and Knowledge*, K. Gunderson (ed.) (Minneapolis: University of Minnesota Press, 1975), and David Wiggins, *Sameness and Substance* (Cambridge, Mass.: Harvard University Press, 1980), chap. 3.

[27] For a further discussion and defense of these ideas see Hoffman and Rosenkrantz, *Substance: Its Nature and Existence*, pp. 91–191.

all living things of the sort in question have a microstructural hereditary blueprint and a vital regulative or controlling part.

The intuitive concept of a *regulating* or *controlling* cause employed in the foregoing discussion plays a role in both ordinary discourse and scientific reasoning. This intuitive causal concept is a concept of a stronger causal relation than either a contributing cause or a causal determinant. Moreover, being a regulating or controlling cause and being a sustaining cause are different relations. For example, the functional activities of a human's central nervous system regulate, directly or indirectly,[28] all of a human's life-processes, whereas the functional activities of a human's heart sustain, but do not regulate, these life-processes.[29]

We concede that the ordinary or scientific concept of a regulating or controlling cause is difficult to analyze. In this respect it resembles many other intuitive causal notions. Nonetheless, this ordinary or scientific concept is a legitimate one, and there is no reason to disallow its use in providing a principle of organization for the parts of an organism.[30]

We are now ready to define our technical conception of one functional thing being *functionally subordinate* to another.

(D9) x is functionally subordinate to y at a time t =df. at t, x is an organic living or functional entity, and y is an organic living or functional entity, and there exists an organism, O, such that: y is a vital proper part of O, and for some time t', later than t, but not so much later than t that O could not live from t until t', (the degree of naturalness of O's life-processes remaining constant from t until t') entails [that from t until t', y has a function, f, and any life-process or functional activity of

---

[28]   *x indirectly regulates y* $\Leftrightarrow$ *x* regulates *y* by regulating some *z*, other than *x* and *y*, which regulates *y*. *x directly* regulates *y* $\Leftrightarrow$ *x* regulates *y*, but not indirectly. For example, by directly regulating the peripheral nervous system, the central nervous system indirectly regulates motions of the arms and legs.

[29]   It should also be noted that possibly, *y* regulates or controls the activities of *x* without *y* sustaining the activities of *x*. For instance, it is logically possible for someone to regulate or control a corporation's activities without sustaining that corporation's activities.

[30]   Of course, it would be a good thing to have an analysis of the ordinary or scientific causal concepts employed in our account. In particular, if we were to possess analyses of the concepts of a sustaining cause and a regulating cause, then it would deepen our understanding of the principle of organization for the parts of an organism. But an inquiry into the nature of these causal concepts falls outside the scope of this paper. Although the application of these causal concepts to particular cases may be imprecise to some degree, their application is sufficiently precise for our purposes.

x occurring at t' is regulated by y's performing f at some time t^* $(t \leq t^* < t')$.]

Observe that (D9) defines a concept of a causal relation which must hold between a master-part of an organism and any part of that organism whose life-processes or functional activities are regulated by that master-part.[31] Ordinarily, in those cases in which y is a master-part which satisfies (D9), y is a system of parts having a joint n-function. For example, in one sort of case y is the central nervous system of a living human being, O, and x is *another* organic living part of O, e.g., O's right lung, which is functionally subordinate to y. In another sort of case, x is *identical* with y. For instance, a human's central nervous system is a master-part of that human, one which is *self-regulating*. Thus, a human's central nervous system is functionally subordinate to itself, and is a limiting case of functional subordination in our technical sense.

We shall call anything which is possibly a part of a living organism a *biotic entity*. Biotic entities may be either non-living entities, e.g., organic macromolecules and water molecules, or organic living entities, e.g., heart cells and hearts.

But suppose that Jones's heart is successfully replaced with a pump made of plastic, rubber, and metal. Is this artificial heart a part of Jones? Does such an artificial heart count as a biotic entity? Such an artificial organ or device is not a biological entity: it is not an entity which is a proper object of scientific inquiry of a distinctively biological sort. After all, a living organism is an entity of a certain *natural kind* whose nature is investigated by an appropriate branch of natural science. Accordingly, it appears that the nature of an organism places certain limitations on what sorts of parts it can have. It seems that one of these limitations is that an organism cannot have an artificial organ or device of the sort in question as a part. By this reasoning, an artificial heart made of plastic, rubber, and metal is not a part of Jones, any more than Jones's eyeglasses are a part of Jones: clearly, both are appliances that are in varying degrees useful to Jones, but Jones's

---

[31] In a case where y is a master-part, x is *ultimately* under the control or regulation of y. However, this is compatible with x's being under the control of another part of O which is not a master-part. For example, consider a functional part, p, of a heart cell, c, which is a part of an organism O. While p may be regulated in part by the nucleus of c, p *ultimately* will also be regulated by a master-part of O. Thus, there may be a hierarchy of control or regulation over a given part of an organism. The relation defined in (D9) is one which *all* of the organic living or functional parts of an organism bear to a controlling or regulating 'master-part.'

nature precludes either of them being a part of Jones. Based upon the foregoing argument, it appears that an artificial heart of this kind is not a biotic entity.

In contrast, given the nature of a human organism, it seems that a human's *biological* heart, kidneys, eyes, lungs, and so forth *are* parts of that human. It is evident that a human's *original* biological organs are parts of that human, and it would appear that a successfully transplanted biological organ, for example, a heart, is also a part of the recipient. But the claim that such an organ is a part of the recipient is not as obvious as the claim that an organism's original biological organs are parts of that organism. Nevertheless, since a biological organ that is successfully transplanted to an organism, O, is an organic living entity that may have a full range of biological activities which are regulated by O's master-part, it is not implausible to suppose that a biological organ of this kind may be a part of O. In any event, we aim to provide a principle of organization for the parts of an organism which is compatible with the possibility of an organism's having a transplanted part.

Every part of an organism, e.g., a heart, must either have a function, or be an organic living entity, e.g., an appendix, or neither, e.g., a mutation such as a non-functional non-living hump. We shall call a living or functional part of an organism a *basic* biotic part, and a non-living, non-functional part of an organism a *non-basic* biotic part. We aim to provide a functional principle of organization for the parts of an organism which accommodates the possibility of both basic and non-basic biotic parts.

The notion of functional unity in question is defined partly in terms of a mereological relation which attaches a non-basic biotic entity to a basic biotic entity. We specify this attachment relation in the following definition:

> (D10) *A non-basic biotic entity, x, is attached to a basic biotic entity, y, at a time t* =df. (i) at t, x is a non-basic biotic entity, and y is a basic biotic entity, and (ii) at t, either x (or a part thereof) and y (or a part thereof) compose a mereological compound in virtue of their being joined, or there is a material object, z, other than any of these entities, such that x (or a part thereof), y (or a part thereof), and z compose a mereological compound in virtue of their being joined and connected.

(D10) presupposes our principle of unity for the parts of a

mereological compound in terms of the parts of that compound being joined and connected.

By utilizing the concept of functional subordination defined in (D9), and the concept of attachment defined in (D10), we formulate our analysis of an organizing causal relation for the parts of an organism as follows:

(D11) Discrete biotic entities $P_1...P_n$ are *functionally united* at a time t =df. (i) at t, some or all of $P_1...P_n$ are basic biotic entities, and there is a P_y, such that each of these basic biotic entities is functionally subordinate to P_y; and (ii) at t, for any one of $P_1...P_n$, P_x, if P_x is a non-basic biotic entity, then P_x is such that: [at t, or an earlier time, some part of P_y, or some part of an organic living or functional entity that is functionally subordinate to P_y, encodes hereditary information which, under the environmental conditions obtaining up to t, is expressed at t by P_x being attached to, or being inside of, some basic biotic entity referred to in (i)];[32] and (iii) at t, there does not exist a biotic entity discrete from $P_1...P_n$ which is functionally subordinate to P_y; there does not exist a biotic entity discrete from P_y to which P_y is functionally subordinate; and there does not exist a non-basic biotic entity discrete from $P_1...P_n$ which satisfies the condition on non-basic biotic entities in the bracketed portion of (ii).

The first clause of (D11) requires that functionally united basic biotic entities are functionally connected in the sense of being functionally subordinated to the same master-part. But the first and second clauses of (D11) also allow for the possibility that biotic entities $P_1...P_n$ are functionally united even if some of $P_1...P_n$ are *not* basic biotic entities. The second clause of (D11) deals with all possible cases of non-basic biotic entities. The third clause of (D11) expresses a maximization requirement which guarantees that functionally unified biotic parts $P_1...P_n$ do not compose an organic living entity which is a mere proper part of an organism. Since (D11) is intended to provide the basis of a principle of organization for the parts of an *organism*, and since a

---

[32] We presuppose the biological notion that a part of an organism encodes hereditary information which is expressed in a particular way under certain environmental conditions. Although this notion stands in need of further analysis, it is clear enough for present purposes.

102   JOSHUA HOFFMAN AND GARY S. ROSENKRANTZ

proper part of an organism cannot qualify as an organism, a guarantee of this kind is required.

Utilizing the conception of functional unity specified in (D11), our proposal is that a satisfactory principle of organization for the parts of an organism is expressed by the following necessary equivalence.

(P_O) (Discrete biotic entities $P_1...P_n$ are organized into an organism at a time t) $\Leftrightarrow$ (at t, $P_1...P_n$ are functionally united).[33]

Department of Philosophy
University of North Carolina at Greensboro
Greensboro, North Carolina, 27402–6170,
USA
j_hoffma@uncg.edu
g_rosenk@uncg.edu

[33] Our account of the functional connectedness of biotic parts has the virtue of being able to explain why a number of causally interrelated living entities fail to compose an organism in a wide variety of possible cases, including cases in which one organism's life-processes are sustained by another organism's life-processes via some artificially engineered connection between them, cases in which a parasite's life-processes are sustained by a host's life-processes, cases in which a symbiont's life-processes and its partner's life-processes are mutually sustaining, cases in which a fetus's life-processes are sustained by the life-processes of the female carrying it, cases in which a number of organisms form a colony, and cases of Siamese twins. For in each of these cases there would not be a master-part which regulates the functions of all of the biotic parts in question. Likewise, since some of the biological functions of the parts of a cancerous tumor are not regulated or controlled by a master-part of the diseased organism, our analysis implies that a cancerous tumor is not a part of the diseased organism, an implication which is intuitively plausible. For a detailed discussion of such cases see Hoffman and Rosenkrantz, *Substance: Its Nature and Existence*, pp. 139–42, and 145–49. A possible case of another sort has been described by Eli Hirsch, who commented on an earlier version of this paper at the 1996 Eastern Division Meetings of the American Philosophical Association in Atlanta, Georgia. In this possible case Bill Clinton is attached to Willard Quine by gluing their brains together. It is clear that this would *not* result in an organism. Our analysis of the causal relation which unites the parts of an organism has the virtue of explaining why this is so. When an organism comes into being it must have a microstructural hereditary blueprint, B, and a master-part, M, such that information indicating the functional and structural specifications of M is included within B, and instructions for implementing B are encoded in the organism's hereditary make-up, that is, in certain organic macromolecules. But if at a time t Clinton were glued to Quine in the way indicated, then at t there would be no such microstructural hereditary blueprint for Clinton's brain glued to Quine's brain, e.g., there would be no blueprint of this kind including the information that these brains are glued together. Thus, Clinton's brain glued to Quine's brain wouldn't be a master-part. A parallel argument implies that a collection of these brains is not a master-part, for there is no such microstructural hereditary blueprint including the information that Clinton's brain and Quine's brain coexist. So, our analysis explains why Clinton glued to Quine in the way indicated would not be an organism: it is because there would be no master-part regulating the functions of both Clinton's parts and Quine's parts.

VI

SAMENESS WITHOUT IDENTITY: AN ARISTOTELIAN SOLUTION TO THE PROBLEM OF MATERIAL CONSTITUTION

Michael C. Rea

Abstract
In this paper, I present an Aristotelian solution to the problem of material constitution. The problem of material constitution arises whenever it appears that an object *a* and an object *b* share all of the same parts and yet are essentially related to their parts in different ways. (A familiar example: A lump of bronze constitutes a statue of Athena. The lump and the statue share all of the same parts, but it appears that the lump can, whereas the statue cannot, survive radical rearrangements of those parts.) I argue that if we are prepared to follow Aristotle in making a distinction between numerical sameness and identity, we can solve the problem of material constitution without recourse to co-location or contingent identity and without repudiating any of the familiar objects of common sense (such as lumps and statues) or denying that these objects have the essential properties we ordinarily think that they have.

I

Ordinary material objects can be characterized in a variety of different ways. Better, they can usually be characterized *as* a variety of different things. For example, a bronze statue can be seen as a statue or a lump of bronze; a tree can be seen as a tree or a heap of cells; a hammock can be seen as a hammock, a piece of rope, or perhaps even a net. The fact that these objects can be characterized in such different ways is due to the fact that their parts are unified in several different ways and we have associated sortal terms with each of the various kinds of unity. For example, the parts of a bronze statue are arranged both statuewise and lumpwise; and because they are arranged in both of these ways at once, we are led to say that they compose a statue *and* that they compose a lump. All of this appears harmless enough on the surface, but difficult philosophical problems lurk just below.

One such problem is the problem of material constitution.

Consider, for example, a bronze statue of ·Athena (call it *'Athena'*). On the pedestal where *Athena* stands, we can identify a statue; we can also identify a piece of bronze; and it seems that we may reasonably ask: 'What is the relationship between the statue and the piece of bronze?' At least one answer is that the piece of bronze *constitutes* the statue: it is the lump of stuff out of which the statue is made. But this answer just raises a further question: 'What is constitution?' Many, at least initially, are inclined to say that constitution is *identity*. After all, there is only one object on *Athena's* pedestal, so *Athena* must be identical with the piece of bronze that constitutes it. But this answer will not do, since statues and pieces of bronze have different persistence conditions: for example, the piece of bronze can but the statue cannot survive being melted down and recast as a statue of Ghengis Khan. The alternative is to say that constitution is *not* identity, but it seems that this answer will not do either. If the statue is not identical with the piece of bronze, then it seems there must be two objects located on Athena's pedestal – but surely there is only one. Thus it is not clear what we should say about the relationship between the statue and the piece of bronze.

Generally speaking, the problem of material constitution arises whenever it appears that an object *a* and an object *b* share all of the same parts and yet are essentially related to those parts in different ways.[1] Scenarios like this are puzzling because we are tempted to say both that *a* is identical with *b* and that *a* is distinct from *b*. The problem is particularly intractable because the intuitions on both sides are deeply entrenched and the options for solving it are limited. I have argued elsewhere[2] that, for any puzzle that raises this problem, there are really only three ways to solve it:

(α) reject the view that if *a* and *b* share all of the same parts then *a* is identical with *b*,

(β) reject the view that if *a* is identical with *b* then necessarily *a* is identical with *b*,

(γ) reject some feature of the story that raises the problem (i.e., deny that *a* exists or deny that *b* exists or deny that *a* and *b* are essentially related to their parts in different ways).

---

[1] I have argued elsewhere (Rea (1995) and (1997)) that the puzzle of the lump and the statue, as well as several other philosophical puzzles (including the Ship of Theseus and the Body-Minus puzzle) are all expressions of one and the same problem.

[2] Rea (1995) and (1997).

None of these options is initially appealing. Each is counterintuitive, requiring us to deny some otherwise plausible claim about familiar objects or the relations they bear to their parts.

There has been a great deal of ink spilled over the past three decades in trying to solve the various puzzles that raise this problem. Despite this fact, however, there is at least one solution that has been almost completely ignored.[3] Virtually everybody writing on the problem of material constitution has assumed that to embrace (α) is to embrace the possibility of there being two distinct material objects in the same place at the same time. In fact, however, this assumption is false. We can accept (α) without accepting the possibility of ·co-location if we are prepared to follow Aristotle in making a distinction between different kinds of numerical sameness. I do not myself endorse this kind of solution (though I have some sympathy for it).[4] My goal is simply to show that there is more to be said on behalf of (α) than most recent writers have acknowledged. If Aristotle's views about sameness are correct, then the problem of material constitution can be solved without denying the necessity of identity, without rejecting any of the features of the stories that raise the problem, *and* without embracing the possibility of there being co-located material objects.

II

Central to our discussion will be Aristotle's notion of 'accidental sameness'. What I propose (speaking now and henceforth as an advocate of the solution described in this paper) is that we understand constitution in terms of this relation. I do not propose to *identify* constitution with accidental sameness; rather, I mean simply to suggest that the two relations may be very much alike in many respects.

The story of accidental sameness begins with some 'kooky objects'.[5] According to Aristotle, when Socrates sits down, something called 'seated-Socrates' comes into existence. Seated-Socrates is an 'accidental unity'. It is not a substance, but (like a

---

[3] I say 'almost' because Nicholas White (1986) describes a solution that appeals to all of the same Aristotelian doctrines that I will be appealing to. The trouble is, it is not clear in the end whether the solution White describes is supposed to be more like the one I am describing, or more like the co-locationist solution that I will be rejecting.

[4] The solution I do endorse is described and defended in Rea (forthcoming).

[5] The label is originally due to Gareth Matthews (1982).

substance) it has a 'hylomorphic' structure: Socrates is the 'matter' and seatedness is the 'form', or unifying principle. It comes into existence when seatedness comes to be (metaphysically) predicated of Socrates; it passes out of existence once Socrates is no longer seated. Accidental sameness is the relation that obtains between Socrates and seated-Socrates for as long as they both exist. It is a relation weaker than strict identity but stronger than co-location.[6]

So says Aristotle. But, as is often pointed out, this feature of Aristotle's ontology is rather difficult for modern readers to take seriously. Neither accidental unities nor the relation of accidental sameness seem to have any place among the familiar objects and relations of contemporary ontologies. Why, then, should we believe in things like seated-Socrates? And what is this mysterious relation of accidental sameness?

The second question is fair, and answering it is my main concern in this section. But the first question is a red herring. The fact is, many of us already believe in things *like* seated-Socrates, and that is why we have the problem of material constitution. For example, we believe in fists and statues, trees and human beings. But, like seated-Socrates, all of these things can be characterized as hylomorphic compounds whose matter is some material object (e.g., a hand, a piece of bronze, or some lump of living tissue) and whose form is some (perhaps very complex) property. Of course, this characterization blurs some important distinctions: it makes it sound as if undetached body parts, artifacts, organisms, and the lumps of matter that constitute organisms are all on a par as objects when in fact they are not (according to Aristotle). But, as even Aristotle would admit, whether or not they are all on a par, we do *believe in* all of these things (that is, we believe that there is *some* sense or other in which each of these things exist.) And my point here is simply that among the things we believe in are things that can be construed as hylomorphic compounds which (i) have as their matter other things that we believe in and (ii) exist only so long as a certain property is predicated of that matter. But to say this is just to say that we believe in (at least some) accidental unities. And if we take our belief in accidental unities seriously – if we do not repudiate such objects by

---

[6] Cf. *Topics* A7, 103a23–31; *Physics* A7, 190a17–21, 190b18–22; *Metaphysics* D6, 1015b16–22, 1016b32–1017a6; *Metaphysics* D29, 1024b30–1.

reducing them to their parts as, say, Peter van Inwagen does[7] – then we find ourselves confronted with the problem of material constitution.

So Aristotle's 'kooky objects' are in fact not so kooky after all. But what of the relation of accidental sameness? How are we to understand it? From the literature on these matters, we learn the following facts about accidental sameness: (i) it is the relation that holds between an accidental unity and its parent substance;[8] (ii) it is neither necessary identity nor contingent identity (because Aristotle tells us that if a and b are accidentally the same, they are in a way the same and in a way different; but if a and b are identical – either necessarily or contingently so – there is no way in which they are different[9]); and (iii) it is a species of numerical sameness: if a and b are accidentally the same, then they are 'one in number', though, according to Aristotle, they are not 'one in being'.[10]

This last point bears some comment. I take it that (roughly speaking), for any a and b, a and b are numerically the same just in case a and b are to be *counted* as one thing. Thus, in saying that accidental sameness is a species of numerical sameness, Aristotle is just saying that accidental sameness is one among several relations whose relata are to be counted as one thing. Now, most contemporary philosophers hold that, for any a and b, a and b are to be counted as one thing just in case a is identical with b. If they are right, then it makes no sense to say that there is a relation which is not identity but which is, nonetheless, a kind of numerical sameness. But I am not convinced that they are right. It certainly is not part of 'common sense' to think that, for any a and b, a and b are to be counted as one thing just in case a is identical with b. As Denis Robinson points out, when we count

---

[7] See van Inwagen (1990), esp. Chapter 10.

[8] I should note that the examples by which Aristotle introduces us to accidental sameness are all examples in which the relata are a genuine substance and a compound whose constituents are that substance and some property such as seatedness. However, I see no reason to suppose that the relation could *not* hold between, say, a piece of bronze and the statue that it constitutes, despite the fact that neither is a genuine substance.

[9] One might object here that objects that are only contingently identical *do* differ in their modal properties, and so accidental sameness is really no different from contingent identity after all. But this misrepresents the contingent identity theorist's view. Contingent identity theorists deny that objects have modal properties. This is what enables them to respect Leibniz's Law while at the same time denying that identity is necessary. (See, for example, Gibbard (1975).)

[10] All of these points are made in Cohen (unpublished), Lewis (1991), Matthews (1982) and (1992), and White (1986). For relevant texts in Aristotle, see note 6.

commonsensically we individuate objects by their matter.[11] When we sell our dining room furniture, for example, we don't charge people for the table, the chairs, *and* the pieces of wood that constitute them. But then why think that philosophers should count things any differently?

The obvious reply is that philosophers make distinctions where common sense does not. The philosopher recognizes that a bronze statue is not *identical* with the piece of bronze that constitutes it; thus, one might argue, she is obliged to count two things where common sense counts only one. But why should we agree with this? Granted, we have strong philosophical intuitions that support:

(1) For any region R, there are (at least) two objects in R just in case $\exists x \exists y(x$ is in R & y is in R & $x \neq y)$.

But we also have strong philosophical intuitions that support:

(2) A statue fills the region occupied by *Athena*; a piece of bronze fills the region occupied by *Athena*; the statue in that region is not identical with the piece of bronze; and only one object fills that region.

If we did not have intuitions that support (2), there would be no problem of material constitution. But, of course, if (2) is true, (1) is false; and I see no obviously compelling reason for preferring (1) over (2).

'But,' you say, 'isn't (2) just unreasonable? How do we count objects if we don't count *two* of them in a region where there is a statue and a piece of bronze distinct from the statue?' Here is what seems to me to be a reasonable answer to this question that is consistent with our common sense counting practices and doesn't entail that (1) is true: We count one object (and only one object) in every region that is filled by matter unified in some object-constituting way. We count one *statue* in every region that is filled by matter arranged statuewise; we count one *lump* in every region that is filled by matter arranged lumpwise; and we count one *object* in every region that is filled by matter arranged in either or both of these ways (or any other object-constituting way). Thus, when we recognize a statue and a lump in a particular region and deny that the statue is identical with the lump, we

---

[11] Cf. Robinson (1985).

are committed to the claim that there is matter in the region arranged both statuewise and lumpwise, and that being a statue is something different from being a lump; but all of this is consistent with there being just one object in the region.[12]

Let us return now to the business of characterizing accidental sameness. Accidental sameness is not identity, but it is a kind of numerical sameness. From this fact it follows (perhaps obviously) that (iv) accidental sameness is not co-location. I take it that, necessarily, if *a* and *b* are numerically the same at a certain time, then *a* and *b* share all of their parts in common at that time. Accidental sameness, then, entails complete community of parts. But co-location does not. For example, an event and a material object can fully occupy the same region of spacetime without sharing all of their parts in common. Likewise (though more controversially) two classes, a class and an event, and perhaps even two events[13] can fully occupy the same region of spacetime without sharing all of their parts in common. Of course, I have turned the discussion so that I am no longer just talking about material objects; but the point here was only to show that co-location does not entail complete community of parts, and that is exactly what these examples show.

So accidental sameness is a relation weaker than identity but stronger than co-location. It occurs whenever some matter is organized in several different ways at once, and whenever it occurs we can identify different kinds of objects in the same place but nevertheless count 'them' as one thing (and rightly so). If there is such a relation, it affords us an easy solution to the

---

[12] One might note here that there is a more direct (and more Aristotelian) argument to be had for the conclusion that we don't have two things in the region filled by *Athena*. According to Aristotle, 'thing' and 'object' aren't genuine count-nouns; thus, the question 'How many *things* (or *objects*) occupy the region filled by *Athena*?' is simply defective. It makes sense to ask how many *statues* fill that region, or how many *lumps* fill that region; but, the answer to each of these questions is obviously just 'one'.

This is all true enough, but I do not think that it renders my remarks about counting objects unnecessary. The reason is that even if Aristotle did not countenance 'object' and 'thing' as count nouns, many philosophers today do. The inference from the fact that there is one statue and one lump (distinct from the statue) completely filling the region occupied by *Athena* to the conclusion that there are two things or two material objects filling that region is not at all uncommon. And those who are inclined to make such an inference are not at all likely to be impressed by one who simply denies that 'thing' and 'object' are count nouns. What we need is some plausible story about counting objects that enables us to count only *one* object in a place where it appears that we should be counting *two* (or more). And that is precisely what I have given.

[13] According to Jonathan Bennett ((1988), p. 124) two chess games can be co-located without sharing all of their parts in common.

problem of material constitution. We can simply say that whenever we have an object a and an object b that share all of the same parts but are essentially related to their parts in different ways, the relevant a and b are numerically the same but not identical. To be sure, this solution carries an intuitive price, but for those who are convinced that identity is necessary, that (say) statues and lumps have different persistence conditions, and that the co-locationist's view does not respect our intuitions about counting, the price may well be worth paying.

III

Now that I have fully described the Aristotelian solution, I would like to close by defending it against four objections. I do not pretend that these are the only objections that could be raised against the view, but they seem to me to be some of the most obvious and therefore the most important.[14]

First objection: In the last section I said that, for any region of space R, there is one statue in R just in case R is filled by matter arranged statuewise; there is one lump in R just in case R is filled by matter arranged lumpwise; and there is *one object* in R just in case R is filled by matter arranged in either or both of these ways (or in any other object-constituting way). I said this to help make the notion of accidental sameness more plausible, but one might wonder whether this view of counting is even *consistent* with the doctrine of accidental sameness. For once we accept this view, it appears that we can give a very straightforward argument for the conclusion that (for example) *Athena* is *identical with* the lump of bronze (call it 'Lump$_A$') that constitutes it. The argument is as follows:

(1) *Athena* is identical with the object whose matter is arranged statuewise.
(2) Lump$_A$ is identical with the object whose matter is arranged lumpwise.
(3) The object whose matter is arranged statuewise is identical with the object whose matter is arranged lumpwise.
(4) Therefore: *Athena* is identical with Lump$_A$.

Obviously, if my remarks about counting commit me to the

[14] I am grateful to Mary Louise Gill and to various members of an audience at the University of Delaware for bringing the first and fourth of these objections to my attention.

premises of this argument, then they entail the denial of the claim that *Athena* and Lump$_A$ bear to one another the relation of accidental sameness.

In fact, however, there is at least one premise in this argument that I am *not* committed to: premise (3). One might think that (3) just follows from the fact that there is *one* object whose matter is arranged both lumpwise and statuewise. But actually (3) follows from this only if Aristotle's views about sameness are false. Numerical sameness, according to Aristotle, does not entail identity. That is, on his view, it does *not* follow from the fact that there is one object whose matter is arranged both lumpwise and statuewise that the object whose matter is arranged lumpwise is identical with the object whose matter is arranged statuewise. Thus it is not my remarks about counting alone that commit me to the conclusion that *Athena* is identical with Lump$_A$, but only the conjunction of those remarks with the claim that Aristotle's views about sameness are false. My remarks about counting *alone* are perfectly consistent with Aristotle's views about sameness.

Second objection: I say that there is one (and only one) object in a region just in case the region is filled by matter unified in any object-constituting way. So, consider a region R that is filled by matter arranged both lumpwise and statuewise. What *is* the object in R? What are its essential properties? If indeed there is just one object in R, these questions should have straightforward answers. But in fact, it seems that they don't (at least not so long as we persist in saying that there is a statue *and* a lump in R). Thus, it seems that, contrary to what I have said, there is not just one object in the region.

This seems to me to be the most challenging objection to this solution. However, the following response strikes me as fairly reasonable: To the first question the correct answer is that the object is both a statue and a lump; to the second question there is no correct answer. According to the view I have been defending, in a region filled by matter arranged both statuewise and lumpwise there is a statue, there is a lump, and the statue is numerically the *same object* as the lump (though it is distinct from the lump). This seems sufficient to entitle us to the claim that the *object* 'is' both a statue and a lump, so long as we don't infer from this that the statue is identical with the lump or that the object has the essential properties of both statues and lumps. Given this view, however, it is hard to see how there could be any correct answer to the question, 'What are its essential properties?' absent information about whether 'it' is supposed to refer to the statue or to the lump. The pronoun is ambiguous, and so we would need to disambiguate it before we could give any sort of straight-forwardly correct answer to the question. Does this imply that there are two objects in the region? It might appear to because we are accustomed to finding pronoun ambiguity only in cases where the pronoun refers to *two* numerically distinct items at once. But if Aristotle's views about sameness are correct, we should expect to find pronoun ambiguity in cases of accidental sameness as well. Thus, to infer from the fact that the pronoun is ambiguous that there must be two objects in the region is simply to *presuppose* that Aristotle's views about sameness are false.

Third objection: Despite what I said in the previous section, one might still have doubts that this solution has any significant advantage over the co-locationist's solution. After all, one of the main selling points for this Aristotelian solution is that it allows us to count *one* object instead of two on *Athena's* pedestal. But is this really enough to justify the whole apparatus of accidental same-ness? Why couldn't the co-locationist just concede that *both* ways of counting (hers and the Aristotelian's) are equally legitimate? Why not just say that it is legitimate to count by identity as the co-locationists do and it is legitimate to count filled regions of space as the Aristotelians do. Doesn't this get us what we want without all of the confusion about different kinds of numerical sameness?

Actually, it doesn't. What is unsatisfying about the co-location-ist's view (to those who *are* unsatisfied about it) is not just the fact that their counting practices are abnormal, but that they seem to be mistaken or even incoherent. For example, Harold Noonan has complained that the co-locationist seems to 'manifest a bad case of double vision';[15] and Peter van Inwagen (in his earlier work, anyway) reports that he simply cannot understand their view.[16] It is not clear what it would be for there to be two material objects in the same place at the same time. It just seems obvious that there is exactly *one* object in a region if and only if there is matter in that region unified in some object constituting way or other. Of course, this is no argument against the co-locationist, and there is nothing to prevent the co-locationist from respond-ing in like kind to the Aristotelian by saying that *she* doesn't understand what it would be for there to be different kinds of

[15] Noonan (1988), p. 222.
[16] Van Inwagen (1981), 128.

numerical sameness. Still, it does explain why the apparatus of accidental sameness is necessary: the co-locationist's way of counting seems to be more than inappropriate; it seems to be mistaken and perhaps incoherent. Thus, if we want to embrace (α) we need some principled reason to avoid counting the way that the co-locationist does, and the doctrine of accidental sameness affords us just such a reason.

Fourth objection: One might have doubts about whether the solution I have been exploring in this paper is really *Aristotelian*, as I have labeled it. For one might think that, instead of solving the problem of material constitution by appeal to accidental sameness, Aristotle would instead have opted for an 'eliminativist' solution. An eliminativist solution is one that denies the existence of at least one of the objects mentioned in every puzzle about material constitution. So, for example, one might think that in the *Athena*/Lump$_A$ example, Aristotle would say that there is no lump; there is only *Athena*. And one might think that Aristotle would say that in the case of a human body and its constitutive lump of tissue, there is again no lump; there is only the body. The reason, in short, is that for Aristotle, forms are hierarchically ordered. So, for example, the form *human being* is a form in the most basic, paradigmatic sense of the term whereas the form *lump of tissue* is not. And the 'form' *statue*, though not a genuine, paradigmatic form, at least has better claim to being called a form than the form 'lump of bronze'. So, one might think that Aristotle would simply recognize the object characterized by the primary form in each case and repudiate the other.

Even if this objection is sound, it does not undermine the main goal of this paper which is simply to present and go some distance toward defending a solution that has been largely ignored in the contemporary literature. But the objection is worth answering since in fact there is good reason for thinking that Aristotle would have embraced the accidental sameness solution that I have been exploring here. On the eliminativist interpretation, Aristotle's ontology faces some difficult questions. For example: Suppose a man *comes to be* from a lump of organic tissue. If the eliminativist view is correct, then the lump of tissue is *destroyed* when the man comes into existence. But then it turns out that change (of that sort, anyway) is merely replacement of one thing by another: there is nothing that persists through, or underlies the change. But in *Physics* A.7 Aristotle seems to deny that substantial change is merely replacement of one thing by another; he explicitly claims that in every such case something *must* underlie the change. Thus, the eliminativist view seems to be in tension with what Aristotle takes to be the correct analysis of change.

Moreover, it seems that the eliminativist view gives Aristotle only an *incomplete* solution to the problem of material constitution. Consider, for example, a hammock which is also a fishnet (and suppose that the artist designed the hammock to serve this dual purpose). We may reasonably suppose that there are some changes that would destroy the fishnet and not the hammock and vice versa; thus we confront the problem of material constitution. Will the eliminativist solution work here? Since neither form seems to be primary, it seems the solution will work only if Aristotle is willing to deny that *both* hammock and fishnet exist. But Aristotle does not seem to want to go to such extremes – at least not if his remarks in *Metaphysics* H.2 are any guide. There, Aristotle countenances all kinds of artifacts: books, caskets, beds, thresholds, and so on. Of course, these are not genuine substances; but for Aristotle, to say that something is not a genuine substance is not at all the same as saying that it does not exist. But if he does not deny the existence of hammocks and fishnets, then he must avail himself of some *other* solution to the problem of material constitution in this case.

In light of these problems, and in light of the fact that Aristotle already believes in the relation of accidental sameness, I find it hard to believe that Aristotle would not have endorsed the accidental sameness solution that I have been exploring in this paper. The accidental sameness solution suffers from none of the problems just mentioned. In the case of a man's coming to be from a lump of tissue, we can say that the lump still exists (and thus underlies the change) though it is not identical with the man: man and lump stand in the relation of accidental sameness (or, at any rate, a relation very much like it). Similarly, we can say that the hammock and the fishnet stand in the relation of accidental sameness (or, again, a relation very much like it). I hasten to point out that here I am stretching the notion of accidental sameness beyond what some would consider to be its 'proper' use. Moreover, I do not deny that the doctrine of accidental sameness faces its own share of difficult questions. But since Aristotle already believes in such a relation, those are questions he faces whether or not he appeals to accidental sameness in order to solve the problem of material constitution. So why wouldn't he appeal to accidental sameness to solve the problem? It seems to me much more reasonable to ascribe to Aristotle that sort of genuine solution to the problem of material constitution than to attribute to him the problematic and incomplete eliminativist solution described above.[17]

Department of Philosophy
University of Delaware
Newark, DE 19716
USA
mcrea@udel.edu

References

Bennett, J. (1988). *Events and Their Names* (Indianapolis: Hackett).
Cohen, S. Unpublished. 'Aristotle's Alternative to Referential Opacity.'
Kim, J. (1966). 'On the Psycho-Physical Identity Theory', *American Philosophical Quarterly* 3: 227 – 235.
Lewis, F. (1991). *Substance and Predication in Aristotle* (New York: Cambridge University Press).
Matthews, G. (1982). 'Accidental Unities,' in *Language and Logos*, edited by M. Schofield and M. Nussbaum (Cambridge: Cambridge University Press), 251–262.
—— (1992). 'On Knowing How to Take Aristotle's Kooky Objects Seriously,' presented at the Pacific Division meeting of the APA, Portland.
Noonan, H. (1988). 'Reply to Lowe on Ships and Structures', *Analysis* 48: 221–223.
Rea, M. (1995). 'The Problem of Material Constitution,' *Philosophical Review* 104: 525–552.
—— (1997). 'Introduction,' pp. xv–lvii in *Material Constitution: A Reader*, edited by Michael C. Rea (Lanham MD: Rowman & Littlefield), 1997.
—— (forthcoming). 'Constitution and Kind Membership' *Philosophical Studies*.
Robinson, D. (1985). 'Can Amoebae Divide Without Multiplying?', *Australasian Journal of Philosophy* 63: 299–319.
van Inwagen, P. (1981). 'The Doctrine of Arbitrary Undetached Parts', *Pacific Philosophical Quarterly* 62: 123–37.
—— (1990). *Material Beings* (Ithaca: Cornell University Press).
White, N. (1986). 'Identity, Modal Individuation, and Matter in Aristotle,' in *Midwest Studies in Philosophy*, vol. 11, *Studies in Essentialism*, edited by P. French *et al.* (Minneapolis: University of Minnesota Press): 475–494.

[17] An earlier version of this paper was read at the 1995 Eastern Division Meeting of the APA in New York City. I would like to thank my commentator, Mary Louise Gill, as well as Michael Bergmann, Michael Loux, Gareth Matthews, Trenton Merricks, Alvin Plantinga, Philip Quinn, and Dean Zimmerman for helpful comments and criticism.

INDEX